IT Service Management: ISO/IEC 20000-1:2018
Introduction and Implementation Guide

Other publications by Van Haren Publishing

Van Haren Publishing (VHP) specializes in titles on Best Practices, methods and standards within four domains:
- IT and IT Management
- Architecture (Enterprise and IT)
- Business Management and
- Project Management

Van Haren Publishing is also publishing on behalf of leading organizations and companies: ASLBiSL Foundation, BRMI, CA, Centre Henri Tudor, CATS CM, Gaming Works, IACCM, IAOP, IFDC, Innovation Value Institute, IPMA-NL, ITSqc, NAF, KNVI, PMI-NL, PON, The Open Group, The SOX Institute.

Topics are (per domain):

IT and IT Management	Enterprise Architecture	Project Management
ABC of ICT	ArchiMate®	A4-Projectmanagement
ASL®	GEA®	DSDM/Atern
CMMI®	Novius Architectuur	ICB / NCB
COBIT®	Methode	ISO 21500
e-CF	TOGAF®	MINCE®
ISO/IEC 20000		M_o_R®
ISO/IEC 27001/27002	**Business Management**	MSP®
ISPL	BABOK® Guide	P3O®
IT4IT®	BiSL® and BiSL® Next	PMBOK® Guide
IT-CMF™	BRMBOK™	Praxis®
IT Service CMM	BTF	PRINCE2®
ITIL®	CATS CM®	
MOF	EFQM	
MSF	eSCM	
SABSA	IACCM	
SAF	ISA-95	
SIAM™	ISO 9000/9001	
TRIM	OPBOK	
VeriSM™	SixSigma	
	SOX	
	SqEME®	

For the latest information on VHP publications, visit our website: www.vanharen.net.

IT Service Management: ISO/IEC 20000-1:2018

Introduction and Implementation Guide
Second edition

Dolf van der Haven

Colophon

Title:	IT Service Management: ISO/IEC 20000-1:2018 Introduction and Implementation Guide - Second edition
Series:	Best Practice
Author:	Dolf van der Haven
Publisher:	Van Haren Publishing, 's-Hertogenbosch-NL www.vanharen.net.
ISBN Hard copy:	978 94 018 0701 2
ISBN eBook (pdf):	978 94 018 0702 9
ISBN ePUB:	978 94 018 0703 6
Editions:	First edition, first impression, August 2019 (ITSM Press) Second edition, first impression, October 2020
Layout and Design:	Coco Bookmedia, Amersfoort-NL
Copyright:	© Van Haren Publishing and Dolf van der Haven, 2019, 2020

Nothing from this publication may be reproduced, recorded in an automated database or published on or via any medium, either electronically, mechanically, through photocopying or any other method, without prior written permission from the publisher.

This publication was produced with the utmost care and attention. Nevertheless, the text may contain errors. The publisher and the authors are not liable for any errors and/or inaccuracies in this text.

Trademark notices:
ITIL® is a registered trademark of AXELOS Limited. All rights reserved.
COBIT® is a registered trademark of ISACA. All rights reserved.
ISO® and IEC® are registered trademarks of ISO and IEC. All rights reserved.
VeriSM™ is a trademark of IFDC. All rights reserved.
CMMI® is a registered trademark of CMMI Institute. All rights reserved.

Table of Contents

1. **INTRODUCTION** 1

2. **SERVICE MANAGEMENT WHY IS IT NEEDED?** 3

3. **THE ISO/IEC 20000 STANDARD** 5
   - 3.1 The ISO/IEC 20000 series of documents 5
   - 3.2 The structure and contents of ISO/IEC 20000-1:2018 6
     - Clause 1 – Scope 6
     - Clause 2 - Normative references 7
     - Clause 3 - Terms and definitions 7
     - Clause 4 - Context of the organization 7
     - Clause 5 – Leadership 7
     - Clause 6 – Planning 8
     - Clause 7 – Support 9
     - Clause 8 – Operation 10
     - Clause 9 - Performance evaluation 13
     - Clause 10 – Improvement 13

4. **IMPLEMENTING THE REQUIREMENTS OF ISO/IEC 20000-1 – GENERAL CONSIDERATIONS** 15
   - Step 1: Education 15
   - Step 2: Management support 15
   - Step 3: Determine the organization's context 16
   - Step 4: Communicate, communicate, communicate! 16
   - Step 5: What do you have in place now? 17
   - Step 6: Gaps, risks and opportunities 17
   - Step 7: Implementation 18
   - Step 8: Operation 18
   - Step 9: Evaluation and improvement 19

5. IMPLEMENTING THE REQUIREMENTS OF ISO/IEC 20000-1 – PRACTICAL GUIDANCE ON DOCUMENTED INFORMATION 21

- 5.1 Clause 4 21
  - 5.1.1 Internal and external issues 22
  - 5.1.2 Interested parties 23
- 5.2 Clause 5 23
- 5.3 Clause 6 24
  - 5.3.1 Risk management 24
  - 5.3.2 Service management objectives 26
  - 5.3.3 Service management plan 26
- 5.4 Clause 7 27
  - 5.4.1 Competence 27
  - 5.4.2 Processes 27
  - 5.4.3 Procedures 28
  - 5.4.4 Knowledge 28
- 5.5 Clause 8 29
  - 5.5.1 Process design 29
  - 5.5.2 Operational planning and control 31
  - 5.5.3 Plan the services 32
  - 5.5.4 Control of parties involved in the service lifecycle 32
  - 5.5.5 Service catalogue management 32
  - 5.5.6 Configuration management 33
  - 5.5.7 Business relationship management 33
  - 5.5.8 Service level management 34
  - 5.5.9 Supplier management 34
  - 5.5.10 Budgeting and accounting for services 35
  - 5.5.11 Demand management 35
  - 5.5.12 Capacity management 35
  - 5.5.13 Change management 36
  - 5.5.14 Service design and transition 37
  - 5.5.15 Release and deployment management 37
  - 5.5.16 Incident management 38
  - 5.5.17 Service request management 38
  - 5.5.18 Problem management 39
  - 5.5.19 Service availability management 40
  - 5.5.20 Service continuity management 41
  - 5.5.21 Information security management 41
- 5.6 Clause 9 42
  - 5.6.1 Internal audit 42
  - 5.6.2 Management reviews 42
- 5.7 Clause 10 43

6. IMPLEMENTING THE REQUIREMENTS OF ISO/IEC 20000-1:2018 RUNNING THE SMS AND THE SERVICES ... 45
- 6.1 Planning ... 45
  - 6.1.1 Planning the SMS ... 45
  - 6.1.2 Planning processes ... 48
  - 6.1.3 Planning working with other parties ... 50
- 6.2 Operating ... 50
- 6.3 Evaluating ... 53
- 6.4 Improving ... 54

7. CERTIFICATION ... 57

8. BEYOND ISO/IEC 20000 ... 59
- 8.1 VeriSM ... 59
- 8.2 The ISMF ... 60

APPENDIX A: ISO/IEC 20000 RESOURCES ... 61

APPENDIX B: DIFFERENCES BETWEEN THE 2011 AND THE 2018 EDITIONS OF ISO/IEC 20000-1 ... 63
- Introduction ... 63
- Management systems standards structure ... 63
- Explanation of differences ... 64
  - General requirements ... 64
  - Service management processes ... 65
  - Operational planning and control ... 66

ABOUT THE AUTHOR ... 69

1 Introduction

The revised standard for service management, ISO/IEC 20000-1:2018, was published in September 2018 and is the third version of the International Standard for service management, replacing the 2011 edition.

ISO/IEC 20000-1 provides requirements for the planning, design, transition, delivery and improvement of a Service Management System (SMS), which is the coordinated set of policies, processes, organizational structures, people, etc. involved in managing services.

This book introduces the ISO/IEC 20000-1 standard as well as providing extensive practical advice on implementing an SMS that conforms to the requirements. It does so by referring to the ISO/IEC 20000-1:2018 documentation toolkit, which is separately available and contains dozens of templates that allow you to provide the documented evidence necessary. This book, however, can also be read without using the templates, or using others in their place.

This book contains the following chapters:
Chapter 2 deals with a general overview of service management and why you need it — services are everywhere, even if you don't realize it.
In Chapter 3, an overview is given of the ISO/IEC 20000-1 standard and the other parts of the ISO/IEC 20000 series.
High-level steps on how to implement the requirements of ISO/IEC 20000-1 are provided in Chapter 4.
Chapter 5 contains the practical guidance for conforming to the requirements of the standard. It extensively details the documented information needed as well as referring to the documentation toolkit developed together with this book.
Chapter 6 highlights the practical aspects of running an SMS beyond the documented information discussed in Chapter 5, instead focusing on planning, running, measuring and improving the SMS and other services.
Chapter 7 provides information on the certification process, in case your organization may want to get formal certification against the standard through external audits.

To conclude, Chapter 8 describes two models that can help you go beyond the requirements of the standard and look at service management from a holistic perspective.

Appendix A lists further resources that may be helpful during your journey in implementing ISO/IEC 20000-1.

Finally, Appendix B lists the main differences between the 2018 edition of the standard and the previous 2011 edition.

Note that the documentation toolkit, containing several dozen templates that can be used to conform to the requirements of the standard, is available from www.vanharen.net.

2 Service management why is it needed?

Services are as old as the world – various forms of services have been around for a long time, including legal services, transport services and governmental services. As a subset, Information Technology (IT) services have been around a bit shorter. IT services importantly gave rise to what was known as IT Service Management (ITSM), because a need was felt better to control these services and the costs of them. ITSM, in turn, has been generalized to general Service Management, by applying its principles to other services than IT. In fact, most, if not all, services today contain some IT component, if even as limited as a payment method or a website. This book, and the ISO/IEC 20000-1 standard, therefore refer to Service Management rather than ITSM, just to show how it can be applied to all types of services.

Contrary to popular belief, service management does not have to be an old-fashioned, rigid framework that slows down every effort in bringing positive changes. This is despite the fact that the fast-paced development of services today, pushed by (and, in turn, leading to) rapidly evolving customer requirements, result in many developers believing that traditional service management needs to make way for "newer" frameworks, such as Lean, Agile, DevOps and other related methodologies. In reality, the new ISO/IEC 20000-1 standard fully supports the use of these newer methodologies, but it can also be used with more traditional approaches to service management.

A standard like ISO/IEC 20000-1 does not prescribe how you should implement your service management processes; it only states what these processes should conform to. This opens up a range of possibilities for organizations to implement their processes in a way that is suited to their circumstances. Even a framework such as ITIL®, which is far more prescriptive, is clear regarding the modification of its processes to the organization's needs. I tend to modify its slogan to *Adapt and Adopt*. You need to be able to adapt your service management practices to your organization's culture and then adopt said practices to maximize the outcome.

You can conform to all requirements of ISO/IEC 20000-1 in various ways, adapted to the management practices you have adopted and the services you provide. It applies to both waterfall-type service implementations and restrictive change management practices, as well as to continuous delivery practices with a rapid change approval turnaround time. It is all dependent on what your service management policy (the high-level statement by which service management is governed) and your principles (the related statements on what is permissible in, for example, change or incident management) are. These, in turn, are dependent on the culture of the organization.

What makes service management so valuable is that it enables a structure for provisioning that can be adapted to the culture of the organization. People working within this structure know the level of flexibility and autonomy needed to make decisions independently for the organization. Customers are aware that they can expect consistent value from the services they purchase, and management know they have a structure in place that promotes efficiency, reduces costs and keeps customers satisfied.

3 The ISO/IEC 20000 standard

■ 3.1 THE ISO/IEC 20000 SERIES OF DOCUMENTS

ISO/IEC 20000 is not a single document — there is actually a series of ten, in which the primary standard (i.e. ISO/IEC 20000-1:2018) is included. ISO decided to distinguish these documents as parts of the 20000 series by assigning numbers to them, hence the primary standard is 20000-1.

Other parts of the 20000 series are as follows:

(Note that with the release of the 2018 edition of Part 1, some dependent parts that are currently published still refer to the 2011 edition and will be updated.)
- ISO/IEC 20000-1 is the international standard for service management, providing requirements to which a service management system (SMS) should conform.
- ISO/IEC 20000-10 (also known as Part 10, and updated in 2018) is the general introduction to the series, containing descriptions of the aims of ISO/IEC 20000, as well as the various other parts and ISO standards related to it. It also contains all terms and definitions used in the series.
- ISO/IEC 20000-2 (Part 2) is a larger document. Part 1 specifies concise and precise requirements that can be audited, whereas Part 2 provides further guidance on how to interpret and implement the requirements.
- ISO/IEC 20000-3 (Part 3) provides guidance on how to define a scope for Part 1: we will see that this is an important aspect in implementing the standard, which may become complex if you are using one or more internal or external suppliers.
- ISO/IEC 20000-5 (Part 5) is an example of an implementation plan for an SMS according to Part 1. As well as a project plan, it also includes guidance on areas such as a business case and templates.
- ISO/IEC 20000-6 (Part 6) provides requirements for certification bodies when they audit an SMS based on ISO/IEC 20000-1. Part 6 is valid for both the 2011 and the 2018 editions of Part 1.

- ISO/IEC 20000-7 (Part 7) provides guidance on the integration and correlation of management systems based on ISO/IEC 20000-1, ISO 9001 (quality management) and ISO/IEC 27001 (information security management).
- ISO/IEC 20000-11 (Part 11) makes a comparison between Part 1 and the Information Technology Infrastructure Library (ITIL).`
- ISO/IEC 20000-12 (Part 12) makes a comparison between Part 1 and the Capability Maturity Model Integration for Services (CMMI®-SVC).
- ISO/IEC 20000-13 (Part 13) makes a comparison between Part 1 and Control Objectives for Information Technology (COBIT®).
- Some parts (4, 8 and 9) seem to be missing from this series; this is due to either cancelling their development, withdrawing or renumbering them.

■ 3.2   THE STRUCTURE AND CONTENTS OF ISO/IEC 20000-1:2018

ISO/IEC 20000-1 is now aligned with the high-level structure and terminology of what is referred to as the "Annex SL", which is an appendix to the ISO Directives. This structure has been, or will be, applied to all management system standards, including the latest editions of ISO 9001 (Quality Management Systems), ISO/IEC 27001 (Information Security Systems), ISO 14001 (Environmental Management Systems) and many others, now also including ISO/IEC 20000-1. Applying the high-level structure results in many requirements being identical or at least very similar right across these standards, making the integration of multiple management systems much easier. If you already have, for example, an ISO 9001:2015 certification, then part of the work you have completed to achieve that can be re-used for your ISO/IEC 20000-1:2018 certification.

This new structure of ISO/IEC 20000-1:2018 is quite different from the 2011 edition, but you will still find similar requirements in both editions, although these will be in different places. If you want to know exactly what has changed between the two editions, refer to Appendix B for an overview.

The high-level structure of these standards is indicated below. In what follows, the specific content of ISO/IEC 20000-1 is described.

Clause 1 – Scope
A general description of what the standard entails. It states that ISO/IEC 20000-1 covers the establishment, implementation, maintenance and continual improvement of an SMS. The standard is applicable to all types of services, be it IT, such as cloud hosting, or non-IT, such as transport or health care. It is also applicable to organizations of any size, ranging from self-employed consultants to large corporations.

Clause 2 - Normative references
This section may contain a reference to other standards that may have to be used in combination with this one. ISO/IEC 20000-1 has no references here, and therefore can be used as a stand-alone standard.

Clause 3 - Terms and definitions
A list of terms used in the standard, defining the context of words such as 'organization', 'service', 'incident', etc. Many of these come from Annex SL, indicated in Clause 3.1, while others have been specifically added for ISO/IEC 20000-1, in Clause 3.2. The list of terms and definitions in ISO/IEC 20000-1 is also identically included in ISO/IEC 20000-10.

Clause 4 - Context of the organization
This is where the actual requirements for the SMS start. This section is mostly based on the default Annex SL requirements, similar to other management system standards.

Clause 4 asks you to perform a number of basic activities to determine the environment that the SMS and services are in. This includes a list of issues both inside and outside of your organization that may have an impact on how you operate the SMS and the services, achieve their objectives and generate value for customers. Issues can be either positive or negative – the possible impact of competition can be an issue, but also the availability of staff in the market.

You should also identify the internal and external stakeholders ("interested parties" in the standard) who have an interest in what your organization does, such as your employees, customers, regulators, HR team, competitors, unions, etc. These groups interact with you and have certain needs and expectations of which you need to be aware.

The third part of this section asks you to define a scope for the SMS, indicating what part of the organization and what services are included. This is a statement similar to the following: *"The SMS supporting the utility services provided by Clean Water, Inc. from Jakarta, Indonesia".* These statements can get quite complex, however, which is why ISO/IEC 20000-3 has been written to guide you through defining the scope of your SMS in more complex cases, such as when you use one or more suppliers to provide your services.

Clause 5 – Leadership
This clause has requirements for the organization's top management, i.e. the people accountable for the SMS, who need to support the establishment of the SMS and provide an appropriate level of involvement to successfully implement and run an SMS that supports the services delivered to the customers.

Leadership support is fundamental to running a successful SMS. Therefore, top management need to explicitly show their involvement in the following areas:

- Making sure a service management policy (stating overall direction for the SMS), service management objectives (stating measurable targets for the SMS) and a service management plan (stating how the SMS is to be implemented and maintained) are created and communicated to all involved parties;
- Making sure third parties involved in the SMS, such as suppliers, are controlled, for instance through the use of service level agreements (SLAs);
- Making sure the SMS meets its objectives and the services meet their outcomes, e.g. by measuring the service management objectives and the customer SLAs;
- Making resources available, such as staff, information, budgets and technical resources, to run the SMS and the services;
- Assigning roles, responsibilities and authorities to the right people who run so they can independently make relevant decisions.

Note that top management is not usually the same as a governing body: the latter is part of larger companies consisting of a board of directors, who have a more strategic role rather than a management one. A governing body would be responsible for governance, including evaluating, directing and monitoring the organization, which top management would implement for them in an operational environment. In smaller companies however, the roles of the governing body and top management may well be fulfilled by the same person(s). Governance of IT is covered in ISO/IEC 38500.

The service management policy is a high-level statement of intention and direction for the SMS and services. It should show commitment to satisfy requirements for the SMS and state support for continual improvement, providing the framework for the service management objectives defined in the next section.

Clause 6 – Planning
This clause contains requirements for the planning of the SMS, including risk management, setting service management objectives and planning to create the SMS itself.

A certain level of risk management is required, albeit not very extensive, to assess risks and opportunities related to the SMS and services. These often follow on from the issues and stakeholders you identified in Clause 4, and should be assessed and treated where required.

Service management objectives need to be set at all levels in the organization, so that everyone involved is aware of the goals of the SMS. The service management objectives state measurable targets for the SMS and the services, being regularly assessed and updated where needed. These can simply be part of the regular performance objectives many organizations already set on an annual basis.

Based on all of the information gathered in Clauses 4 to 6, you can now plan the actual SMS. This should be documented in a service management plan, containing the list of services, any restrictions and obligations, authorities assigned to support the SMS, resources needed and the way in which the success of the SMS is going to be measured, assessed and improved. This helps people working in the SMS to understand its purpose and deliver the services.

Clause 7 – Support
After going through the preceding clauses, the organization has reached the stage where the support needed for the SMS and the services can be determined. This includes the requirements for communication, competency, knowledge, awareness, providing resources for the SMS and creating and maintaining documentation for it. This section also contains a list of key documentation needed for the SMS, although there is more required in Part 1.

Resources need to be made available to support all phases of the lifecycle of the SMS and services. These not only include human resources, but also financial, technical and information ones.

The competence of people supporting the SMS and the services needs to be planned, assessed and managed to ensure proper operation, whilst education and experience should be increased where required: the right person needs to perform the right job.

All people working in the context of the SMS need to gain awareness of the service management policy, objectives and services, so that they have direction for their own activities, are motivated, and understand how best to provide support.

Communication is central to any well-functioning organization. You need to determine what to communicate at what time, as well as how and to whom, so that all relevant stakeholders are aware of what is expected from them.

Service management, even with an Agile approach, does not work well without some level of documentation: this is to not only prove how well your SMS is functioning, but more importantly to lay a foundation for the work people are doing. Service documentation in relation to policies, objectives, processes and reports need to be created, maintained and controlled so that it can be referred to as the agreed way to develop, support and improve the SMS and the services.

The final subject covered in this section is knowledge: you should determine what knowledge is required to support the SMS and the services, making sure it is available and accessible to the people who need it. Knowledge may include documentation, such as design specifications, or databases with incident tickets, for example. This supports the effective operations of the SMS and the services by enhancing collaboration and knowledge-sharing. For example, service documentation is necessary for customers to make use of self-service facilities, so it can be ensured the SMS is well operated and accessible.

Clause 8 – Operation
This clause contains all requirements for what can be recognized as the main service management processes. It is by far the largest section in the standard, as it has extensive requirements for the following processes and activities:
- **Operational planning and control**: this area requires you to control all processes needed to meet the requirements of the SMS and the services, including those that are outsourced to third parties. It is to be done in alignment with the service management plan (described in Clause 6.3) in conjunction with others so that service requirements are met, and the service management objectives (described in Clause 6.2) are achieved.
- **Service delivery**: asks you to coordinate the activities and resources needed to operate the SMS and the services.
- **Plan the services**: deals with determining service requirements, identifying services based on their criticality and aligning them with the service management policy, objectives and requirements. The aim is to plan the services effectively, so that the business objectives of the service provider and the outcomes of the SMS are achieved.
- **Control of parties involved in the service lifecycle**: this section is important in that it requires you to control the services, components or processes that you may have outsourced to others, while retaining accountability for the whole SMS and service lifecycle end-to-end. This ensures that all processes and services generate their desired outcomes and that the service management objectives are achieved. It is made explicit that not all elements in scope of your SMS may be outsourced: you need to at least achieve the requirements in Clauses 4 and 5 yourself; requirements in Clauses 6 to 10 may be achieved with the help of third parties.
- **Service catalogue management**: create a catalogue listing the services, their outcomes and any dependencies, for the benefit of both your internal organization and your customers' expectations. You can create multiple service catalogues for different audiences, such as an internal one and a customer-facing one.
- **Asset management**: this clause has a single requirement which is to identify the assets needed for provisioning the services (such as hardware, software, people, and real estate) and making sure they are managed to meet service requirements and obligations such as the legal and contractual requirements.
- **Configuration management**: this applies to those elements of the services that need to be controlled throughout their lifecycle, known as configuration items (CIs). CIs can, for example, be servers, software, trucks, and other vital parts of the service you are providing. You need to maintain the configuration information of these items so that the information can be used by other processes, such as incident and change management.

- **Business relationship management**: this refers to the process of setting up communications between your organization and customers to ensure the needs and business outcomes are known and met by the services. Reviews are to be held to look at the trends of the service performance and whether outcomes are achieved; measuring customer satisfaction and complaints handling are also part of this area.
- **Service level management**: service level agreements (SLAs) should be established between the service provider and the customers, based on the agreed service requirements, so that agreed service levels can be maintained.
- **Supplier management**: suppliers, who can be internal, external or customers acting as a supplier, need to be controlled to make sure services are provided in a seamless manner. Contracts are set up with external suppliers and documented agreements are set up with internals or customers acting as suppliers. The performance targets for suppliers need to be kept aligned with the SLAs agreed with customers: otherwise you may not be able to meet the SLAs due to the fact that suppliers are held to more relaxed targets than what you have agreed with your customers.
- **Budgeting and accounting for services**: this clause should be part of the overall financial management practices of your organization, but specifically applied to the services. The standard asks you to keep track of the costs made in the SMS against the budget allocated to it in order to control the total finances and be able to make decisions based on the financial performance of the services.
- **Demand management**: requires you to keep track of the demand for your services. This process works closely with capacity management, which is used to adjust the service to meet the demand for it.
- **Capacity management**: the capacity of resources supporting the services needs to be sufficient to meet the service requirements, both at present and in the future, and should therefore be measured and adjusted where required. This not only includes technical capacity (such as bandwidth), but also human (the number of people employed on a service desk), financial (budget needed to refresh computers) and information (capacity of the database behind a ticketing system) resources. This links back to the requirements for resources in Clauses 5 and 7.
- **Change management**: this process is critical to controlling the services appropriately by controlling changes made to them without causing unwanted service outages or reduction in quality. Accordingly, it requires a policy of its own to outline the types of changes (e.g. standard, major, minor, emergency) as well as how best to manage them based on the service provider's direction (including flexibility in who can approve changes). Change requests should be properly initiated, evaluated and approved before being carried out via release and deployment management. This ensures stability of the services.
- **Service design and transition**: this area focuses on managing requests for changes to existing or new services which are categorized in the change management policy as requiring a project, due to their potential impact on customers or existing services. It ensures that these can be delivered and managed within budget with the agreed service quality, including all removal and transfer of services to other providers as

well. This process has a project lifecycle to exercise additional control, including planning, designing, building and transitioning the service into the live environment. It is very closely associated with change, configuration and release and deployment management.
- **Release and deployment management**: this set of activities is where the changes are deployed into the live environment, often based on approved change requests from change management, or pre-approved service requests (e.g. password resets). It can be for a single change or a group of changes batched together into a single release. The aim is to control these activities so that new releases are implemented without unplanned interruption to the services.
- **Incident management**: interruptions to services happen, both due to human error and to technological issues, and therefore need to be properly handled in terms of recording, prioritization and resolution. The aim of incident management is to get the service back up and running as quickly as possible without necessarily finding or fixing the underlying cause – determining the cause of an outage is part of problem management. Major incidents require their own procedure, with more attention from top management.
- **Service request management**: service requests are activities that can be handled without going through the full change management process, such as information or access requests, or pre-approved changes. Password resets, requests for access to systems, and requests for documentation or other information are all part of this. These requests need to be handled efficiently in relation to recording, prioritization and fulfilment so that users continue to benefit from the services.
- **Problem management**: a problem is the cause of one or more actual or potential incidents and, as such, problem management is closely related to incident management. It exists to identify and analyze the root causes of problems and make sure they don't create incidents that impact services in the future. As with incidents and service requests, problems need to be recorded, prioritized and resolved, and it may be necessary to raise a change request to fix the cause.
- **Service availability management**: the availability of the services is considered the main requirement from customers, hence why any risks to this need to be recorded and handled to ensure continual use. Availability should be monitored and compared to what was originally agreed in the service targets.
- **Service continuity management**: similar to availability, risks to continuity of the services need to be identified to ensure customers can use the services. A service continuity plan needs to be created to cater for major outages — this can be part of an overall business continuity plan.
- **Information security management**: information security is, in a broader sense, the subject of ISO/IEC 27001. The requirements in ISO/IEC 20000-1 are, in comparison, much lighter. There needs to be an information security policy providing direction on how the confidentiality, integrity and availability of information used by the services and in the SMS are to be assured. Performing an information security risk assessment leads to setting controls that aim to make sure information is kept secure at all times,

for instance through physical security measures (using badges for building access) or logical security (implementing firewalls and cyberattack prevention measures). Information security incidents are to be handled in similar ways as other incidents, but taking the impact on the information security risk into account.

Clause 9 - Performance evaluation
The requirements in this clause cover the evaluation of the SMS, including measuring, undertaking a management review, carrying out an internal audit and reporting. This section is primarily Annex SL-based, but ISO/IEC 20000-1 adds a number of requirements that are specific to service reporting. Overall, the aim is to monitor, measure, analyze and evaluate the SMS so that it can be managed effectively and support the organization.

Aspects of the SMS and the services, such as service level targets or process efficiency, need to be measured, monitored and reported on. This serves as part of the input for a regular review meeting, which is a chance for top management to assess the state of the SMS and the services from various perspectives in order to make beneficial decisions. Any required changes, risks or opportunities for improvements in the SMS or the services should be discussed as part of this review.

An internal audit program is necessary to regularly assess the SMS and provide information on whether it meets the standard's requirements or any other requirements the organization has for it. This audit should be performed by someone who is sufficiently independent of the area that is being audited to prevent bias during the assessment.

Finally, service reporting needs to be implemented to show how well the SMS and services are performing. This information can then be used by several stakeholders in order to make appropriate decisions, such as increasing the capacity of the services or creating new ones.

Clause 10 – Improvement
This clause focuses upon ways in which the SMS can be improved, such as dealing with nonconformities and ensuring continual improvement.

Nonconformities, i.e. anything that deviates from meeting requirements in Part 1 or the organization's own requirements for the SMS, need to be identified, analyzed and corrected. Actions should be taken to prevent any recurrence and ensure continued performance of the SMS.

Continual improvements should be implemented so that value creation for the customer is ensured, and these should be carried out using specific targets (related to quality, performance or cost etc.) which are to be measured and reported on. Various methodologies can be used for improvement such as Lean, Six Sigma®, the Deming Cycle (Plan-Do-Check-Act, PDCA), etc.

4 Implementing the requirements of ISO/IEC 20000-1 – general considerations

The implementation of an SMS can be seen as a project that needs a certain timeframe within which the objectives are to be realized. At the same time, however, it should not be seen as a project that needs to cover all requirements of ISO/IEC 20000-1 from day one: you should set realistic targets in shorter time boxes and work towards a full implementation via a step-by-step, iterative approach. The framework for the project as a whole is described below as a nine-step program.

■ STEP 1: EDUCATION

First, read the standard ISO/IEC 20000 Parts 1, 2 and 3, to familiarize yourself with the objectives. These documents contain a formal requirement and guidance to establish an SMS, so they should be your permanent reference when starting your journey.

A good training course will take you through Part 1 in detail to help you understand the requirements — there are several training providers and curricula out there that can be used.

■ STEP 2: MANAGEMENT SUPPORT

It is of vital importance to make sure that your top management supports your efforts in implementing the requirements of ISO/IEC 20000-1 as they have a number of important responsibilities in the standard, including:
- Defining a service management policy, expressing general direction for the SMS in line with the organization's strategy;
- Defining or approving service management objectives, which are the organization-wide targets for SMS and the services;
- Making resources available for the design, implementation and support of the SMS. This includes financial, human, and technological information;

- Assigning responsibilities to people for managing the SMS;
- Making sure the SMS achieves its intended outcomes.

As can be seen, these are fundamental aspects that top management needs to be involved in, otherwise the project aimed at achieving compliance with ISO/IEC 20000-1 is going to have serious issues. Without top management support, the implementation of an SMS cannot be successful.

■ STEP 3: DETERMINE THE ORGANIZATION'S CONTEXT

Another fundamental starting point for establishing an SMS is to determine the context of the organization. Using the outputs from a Strengths-Weaknesses-Opportunities-Threats (SWOT) analysis and a Political-Economic-Social-Technological-Legal-Environmental (PESTLE) analysis for example, you can determine relevant aspects of the context of your organization:
- Any issues that are relevant to it, such as competition, resourcing, market developments, new product developments, etc.;
- Relevant stakeholders (a.k.a. Interested Parties) who have an interface with the organization and certain expectations of its activities.
- The internal and external environment in which the organization works, including the influences on the SMS and the services of these environments.

This will help to establish the exact scope of the SMS — a description of what is included and what is not included. A scope description can be as simple as:

The service management system of HappyChick providing egg-transport services from Groenekan, The Netherlands.

However, when providing multiple services, from various locations, using multiple suppliers and having multiple customers, the scope statement can become harder to pin down. For this purpose, ISO/IEC 20000-3 has been written, since it provides more depth on what you should think of when determining the scope of your SMS.

■ STEP 4: COMMUNICATE, COMMUNICATE, COMMUNICATE!

Communication with stakeholders is absolutely crucial for a project like implementing an SMS. You have already determined who your stakeholders are in the previous step and communication needs to be adapted based on whether they are internal or external to your organization, what role they have and their need to know.

ISO/IEC 20000-1 is explicit in what needs to be covered in terms of communication, including:
- Creating awareness of the service management policy and objectives, as well as how they can contribute to the success of the SMS;
- Determining what needs to be communicated, to whom and how, related to anything that is relevant for the SMS and the services;
- Documenting policies, processes, procedures and any other information that needs to be available for the people working in scope of the SMS or other stakeholders.

■ STEP 5: WHAT DO YOU HAVE IN PLACE NOW?

Most likely, if you are a service provider, you already have many aspects in place that ISO/IEC 20000-1 requires. Think of some basic processes to interact with customers, deal with incidents, a service catalogue, etc. You may or may not have documented any of these, but the realization that you already have these aspects in place is the first step towards building a more complete SMS. You should create a baseline of these aspects, as they will form the foundation for your SMS from which you can expand to the full scope of the standard.

■ STEP 6: GAPS, RISKS AND OPPORTUNITIES

Based on this baseline, you need to carry out a gap analysis: read the standard carefully and for each requirement, determine whether you believe you are already meeting that requirement or not. This can result in a checklist in which you indicate what actions you need to take to meet the requirements. Table 1 is a simple example of such a gap analysis.

Table 1. Example gap analysis table

Clause	Met (Y/N)	Action	Owner
4.1 The organization shall determine external and internal issues that are relevant to its purpose and that affect its ability to achieve the intended outcome(s) of its SMS.	N	Create list of internal and external issues and their impact on the SMS.	DvdH
4.2 The organization shall determine: a) The interested parties that are relevant to the SMS and the services; b) The relevant requirements of these interested parties.	Y	List of interested parties and their requirements exists.	N/A
…			

It is likely that this exercise and the previous steps will lead to the identification of risks and opportunities. ISO/IEC 20000-1 does not require a full, formal risk management process (such as in ISO/IEC 27001), but you do need to be aware of the risks that may impact achieving SMS outcomes. You need to document the approach to risk management together with the risk acceptance criteria, determine actions to treat these risks and identify the effectiveness of these actions.

If you have an existing full risk management process, you can also use this to deal with risks related to your SMS.

■ STEP 7: IMPLEMENTATION

Using the gap analysis that you undertook in the previous step, you can now take gradual actions to build your SMS based on the requirements arising out of the standard. You will have identified all actions that you need to perform in order to meet these requirements. Some will be easier than others, so do prioritize and take your time to implement them. A large part will be the actual design of your service management processes.

When designing these processes, use a methodology that ensures the following:
- Make them as efficient as possible, and limit waste where possible— Lean methodologies such as value stream mapping will help here;
- Make sure you understand how processes interact: the output of one process often serves as the input to another, creating a whole system of processes that interact. There are ways to visualize this (such as the Lean system map) and it is likely, if the resulting picture appears complex, that there is room for improvement;
- Establish performance targets for processes and find ways to measure their efficiency. This will form input for the Operation as well as the Evaluation and Improvement steps described below.

Don't forget consistently to communicate with all parties involved (see step 3) during the process of setting up your service management processes. You need to make it clear how these changes are going to improve the way of working in your organization and the customer experience that is provided.

■ STEP 8: OPERATION

The SMS and the services are now in steady state, but this does not mean that they can manage themselves: you need to maintain your service levels and keep your customers happy. Keeping a close watch on these issues can only be done by monitoring and measuring your SMS and services and reporting on them. This includes the process effectiveness, attainment of the service management objectives, customer satisfaction, etc. Only when you do this, do you know if your SMS is running well or not and what improvements you have to make, if any.

■ STEP 9: EVALUATION AND IMPROVEMENT

This final step consists of a number of elements from Clauses 9 and 10 of the standard:
1. Set up an internal audit program — bring in someone who is independent (e.g. from outside the organization that is in scope of the SMS or from another part of the organization). Get them up to speed with the internal audit procedures described in ISO/IEC 20000-1 Clause 9.2 and ISO 19011 [14] and have them periodically (e.g. annually) do an audit of the SMS. Their audit report will feed into the improvement process, the management review and the external auditor's activities.
2. Top management should regularly review the workings of the SMS, say twice a year. They are accountable for what is happening with the SMS and the services, and therefore they need to be informed about them. The aim of the management review is to ensure the continued suitability, adequacy and effectiveness of the SMS and the services.
3. Handle nonconformities — a nonconformity is any non-fulfilment of a requirement, whether these are requirements from ISO/IEC 20000-1 or from the organization's SMS. If they are not conformed to, action needs to be taken to remediate the situation. If a service is not performing according to the agreed service targets, this is usually handled through the incident management process.
4. Set up a Continual Service Improvement (CSI) process — the reason for using the ITIL expression for continual service improvement here is because it is a well-known concept. This CSI program, however, needs to involve both the services and the SMS itself. It should be possible for any stakeholder to submit improvements for management consideration. Moreover, improvements can be triggered by, for example, audits or the risk management process.

Note that ISO has now published the publication *A Practical Guide - ISO/IEC 20000-1 - IT Service Management*, which is a handbook providing guidance for organizations who are new to the standard and are seeking advice and tools to implement their SMS. It contains additional guidance that is not covered in this guide.

5 Implementing the requirements of ISO/IEC 20000-1 – practical guidance on documented information

This chapter provides practical guidance on how to implement and document the requirements of ISO/IEC 20000-1. It shows ways to conform to them and refers to document templates from the ISO/IEC 20000-1:2018 Documentation Toolkit where possible. This is done in a clause-by-clause manner based on the text of the standard.

In many cases the guidance goes beyond the strict requirements of the standard and is based on good practice from a more general point of view. For example, the risk register in the Documentation Toolkit is quite a bit more extensive than strictly required by the standard. However, in practice, the full extent of it will generally benefit the organization and make integration with other management system standards easier.

A distinction is made between both mandatory and non-mandatory documented information: the mandatory documentation is explicitly mentioned in the standard as having to be available. The non-mandatory documentation is mentioned in the standard in phrases such as, "the organization shall determine…" or, "the organization shall ensure…" without an explicit requirement to have this available. These non-mandatory documents have been made available in the Documentation Toolkit anyway, as it will benefit the organization to document these items and auditors will often ask for some sort of evidence of conformance with these requirements.

■ 5.1 CLAUSE 4

Mandatory documented information

Clause	Document	Template
4.3	Scope Statement	4.3 Scope.docx

The scope statement is the only mandatory documented information to be supplied in Clause 4's requirements. In its simplest form, it is a single sentence indicating what is included in the scope of the SMS: mentioning the organization's name, type of services supplied, locations where services are provided and, possibly, specific customers to whom the services are provided.

The toolkit document is a bit more extensive than this: it includes an introduction, reference to terms and definitions, policies, an organization chart, the scope statement itself, and considerations of future scope changes. This information is not all mandatory, but is useful to have included.

Non-mandatory documented Information

Clause	Document	Template
4.1	Issue Tracker	4.1 Internal and External Issue Tracker.xlsx
4.2	Interested Parties	4.2 Interested Parties.xlsx

5.1.1 Internal and external issues

The requirement for the organization to "determine internal and external issues that are relevant to its purpose" can simply result in a list of issues as a result of a SWOT analysis and/or PESTLE analysis.

A SWOT analysis is an overview of an organization's internal Strengths and Weaknesses, and external Opportunities and Threats. Figure 1 illustrates this.

Strengths	**Opportunities**
Examples: expertise, reputation, cost level, technology, etc.	Examples: new technology, new markets, lack of competition, new services, etc.
Weaknesses	**Threats**
Examples: service limitations, understaffing, marketing issues, etc.	Examples: new competition, government and regulatory issues, economy, etc.

Figure 1. SWOT analysis

A PESTLE analysis looks at the context of the organization in terms of Politics, Economy, Social, Technological, Legal and Environmental aspects:
Political aspects: Government policies; wars, terrorism and conflicts; inter-country relationships; bureaucracy.
Economic aspects: Local economy; taxes; international trade; seasonality.

Social aspects: Brand, company, technology image; ethical issues; culture; media views; demographics.
Technological aspects: Emerging technologies; competitor technology development; market readiness.
Legal aspects: Current and future legislation; regulatory bodies; competition law; industry regulations.
Environmental aspects: Environmental regulations; ecology; sustainability.

The output of the SWOT and PESTLE analysis will produce a list of issues or factors that can be positive or negative, internal or external and that can be maintained as a simple list.

The *Internal and External Issues Tracker* template is a more extensive version of this list, including more formal registration of these issues and any indication of follow-up actions and owners where necessary. Given that issues may eventually become risks or improvement opportunities, a possible link to the respective registers for those has been provided as well.

5.1.2 Interested parties
The list of interested parties can contain three columns:
1. The name of the interested party – these can be either internal groups with some interest in your SMS (such as Human Resources, Finance, Sales, Security) or external ones (such as customers, suppliers, regulatory bodies).
2. The interface between your organization and the interested party – typically a named person or a system through which communication is carried out.
3. The reason why the party is interested – what are the requirements from all these parties for your SMS and services?

Examples are provided in the toolkit template.

■ 5.2   CLAUSE 5

Mandatory documented information

Clause	Document	Template
5.2	Service Management Policy	5.2 SM Policy.docx

The service management policy can be a fairly short document, stating the organization's commitment to service management, establishing principles for a framework of setting service management objectives, committing to fulfilling the requirements contained in ISO/IEC 20000-1, and committing to performing continual improvement of the SMS and the services.

The template can be used as is, or be altered as required to reflect service management principles used in your organization.

Make sure this policy is available to all relevant parties, both inside and outside your organization, for as far as they are stakeholders in the services.

Non-mandatory documented information

Clause	Document	Template
5.3	Roles, Responsibilities and Authorities	5.3 RRA.docx

The overview of roles, responsibilities and authorities for running the SMS can in practice be contained in the job descriptions of relevant personnel. If you want to highlight specific roles and make their responsibilities, authorities and qualifications explicit, then you can use the template document as an example to work from.

■ 5.3 CLAUSE 6

Mandatory documented information

Clause	Document	Template
6.1	Risks	6.1 Risk Register.xlsx 6.1 Risk Register - Basic.xlsx
6.1	Impact of Risks	6.1 Risk Register.xlsx 6.1 Risk Register - Basic.xlsx
6.1	Risk Acceptance Criteria	6.1 Risk Management Framework.docx
6.1	Risk Management Approach	6.1 Risk Management Framework.docx
6.2	Service Management Objectives	6.2 SM Objectives.docx
6.3	Service Management Plan	6.3 SM Plan.docx

5.3.1 Risk management

Risk management in ISO/IEC 20000-1 is not a very heavy process. What needs to be documented is limited to risks related to the organization; not meeting the service requirements; and the involvement of other parties in the service lifecycle. The impact upon the customers of these risks for the SMS and the services needs to be determined, together with a risk acceptance criteria (also known as risk appetite) as well as the requirement to document the approach on how to deal with them.

Note that in other parts of the standard, additional risks need to be identified, which may as well be included in this phase: these include risks to service availability, risks to service continuity and information security risks.

Two *Risk Register* Templates are provided: a basic one with only the mandatory fields and an extended one that contains much more information that can also be used for risk management in ISO/IEC 27001 (for example). The risk register provided is a general operational risk management tool suitable for a broader risk management approach than required by the ISO/IEC 20000-1 standard. It is a straightforward spreadsheet that uses the following information:

1. Date when risk got opened.
2. Name of risk.
3. Description of risk.
4. Reference number.
5. Date of last update.
6. Relevant ISO standard (20000-1 in this case).
7. Owner of risk – the person who needs to act.
8. Management reviewed – indicator of whether (top) management has reviewed the risk. They are the ones who can determine the treatment or acceptance of risks.
9. Impact if risk occurs – on a scale from 1 (Low) to 5 (High).
10. Likelihood that risk occurs – on a scale from 1 (Low) to 5 (High).
11. Risk – calculated as Impact x Likelihood, so on a scale from 1 to 25.
12. Risk level – High, Medium or Low, based on the risk calculated under item 11.
13. Treatment – this is the approach taken for this risk. Typically, you can choose from: Accept (i.e. do nothing and hope that the risk does not occur); Reduce (reduce the likelihood or impact of the risk by implementing controls); Transfer (find someone else who is willing to accept the risk as their own).
14. Action plan – this is a log of activities performed to treat the risk.
15. Due date – date on which the risk is expected to be treated.
16. Completion date – actual date on which treatment has been completed.
17. Status – open or closed.
18. Post action plan impact – same as Impact (9) field, but now recalculated after the risk has been treated. This should therefore be lower than the original value, unless the risk has been accepted.
19. Post action plan likelihood – same as Likelihood (10) field, but now recalculated after the risk has been treated. This should therefore be lower than the original value, unless the risk has been accepted.
20. Post action plan risk – same as Risk (11) field, but now recalculated after the risk has been treated. This should therefore be lower than the original value, unless the risk has been accepted.
21. Post action plan residual risk level – same as Risk Level (12) field, but now recalculated after the risk has been treated. This should therefore be lower than the original value, unless the risk has been accepted.

The risk acceptance criteria and the risk management approach can be simply documented, and once again, the exact criteria and approach will vary between organizations so you can make this as complex as you like. The template provided is called the *Risk Management Framework*, which includes both. It is an example of how you can set up a risk management framework, but should be tailored to the needs of your organization.

Non-mandatory documented information
Risk management is a broad area. ISO/IEC 20000-1 is not very demanding when it comes to risk management (compared to e.g. ISO/IEC 27001). There is a lot of literature regarding how to efficiently handle risk management, although it goes beyond the requirements of the ISO/IEC 20000-1 standard. The International Standard for risk management is ISO 31000, with many examples of approaches described in ISO 31010. All sorts of additional documented information may be necessary based on the exact risk management approach you decide to take. These are all optional from the perspective of ISO/IEC 20000-1.

5.3.2 Service management objectives
Service management objectives can be defined as part of an annual performance objectives cycle and should be set at various levels of the organization and for the relevant functions. Objectives should be based on the framework set in the service management policy discussed previously, and they should be SMART – Specific, Measurable, Attainable, Realistic and Time-bound.

The template is just a free-form document with a couple of high-level service management objectives that need to be translated into objectives for specific functions within the organization. It is advisable to communicate the high-level objectives to the relevant parties both inside and outside of the organization.

5.3.3 Service management plan
The service management plan is a high-level document describing what is required to run the SMS and provide the services. It contains eight sections as follows:
1. A list of services: list of your services in scope of the SMS.
2. Limitations: a list of limitations, such as the geographical scope, staff working hours, financial situation, specific customer requirements, etc.
3. Obligations: a list of obligations, such as relevant policies, standards, legal, regulatory and contractual requirements, and how these obligations apply to the SMS and the services.
4. Authorities and responsibilities for the SMS and the services: these will usually have been documented in the Roles, Responsibilities and Authorities document from Clause 5.1.
5. Resources: a list of resources required, such as the number of personnel, knowledge management system, documentation, servers, desktop computers, network infrastructure, cloud infrastructure, budget, etc.
6. Approach for working with other parties involved in the service lifecycle: you should describe here what other parties you use to provide services, including outsource and/

or offshore partners, suppliers (both internal and external ones), customers acting as suppliers, etc. Be specific about the scope of what is provided or operated by these parties and what controls you have put in place to make sure they provide what is necessary. Mention contracts, SLAs, performance indicators and other controls.
7. Technology: describes what technology is needed to run the SMS. This is likely already covered in the "Resources" section, but any specifics can be mentioned here.
8. Measurements and Improvements: this section documents what measurements are taken of the SMS and the services to verify that everything is running optimally. They should be used for (internal) audit purposes, reporting to top management and other stakeholders, and as input to the continual improvement process. Be clear about the tools, technology and human resources needed to achieve this, as well as how regularly reports and audits will be created depending on the audience.

■ 5.4 CLAUSE 7

Mandatory documented information

Clause	Document	Template
7.2	Competence	7.2 Competence.xlsx
7.5	Processes	7.5 Process Template.docx
7.5	Procedures	7.5 Process Template.docx
7.6	Knowledge	N/A

5.4.1 Competence
You need to determine what *competence* personnel working within the context of the SMS need, making sure it is also obtained by them through e.g. education and training. This competence can range from technical skills, communicative abilities, product and service knowledge, process and procedural knowledge to other types of competence. It can be obtained via internal or external training, self-study, consultation of documented processes or procedures, etc. Often, organizations have some form of training database where this can be recorded. The template provided is a simple spreadsheet where for each employee, their name, hiring date, training and completion date of training can be recorded. Note that a distinction has been made between "required" courses (Column K), which would be on the curriculum for a certain role, and "non-required" courses, which would be additional ones followed outside the curriculum.

5.4.2 Processes
All processes required by the standard are to be documented and a *Process template* for process documentation is provided in the toolkit. The elements of this will be described in full detail under Section 5.5 Clause 8, as that is where most processes in the standard are described.

5.4.3 Procedures

Procedures can be written as step-by-step work instructions or by using screenshots from an application. The Process Template contains a section where these procedures can be described. See section 5.5 for details.

5.4.4 Knowledge

Knowledge exists in many forms and formats, ranging from training materials to process documents, incident and problem records to corporate policies. Given that this is such as broad area, no specific template has been provided in the toolkit to cover this section. It is up to the individual organization to make sure knowledge is actually documented and does not merely exist within the heads of individual employees.

Non-mandatory documented information

Clause	Document	Template
7.4	Communication Plan	7.4 Communication Plan.xlsx
7.5.1	Documented information determined by the organization as being necessary for the effectiveness of the SMS	NA
7.5.3	Documented information of external origin determined by the organization to be necessary for the planning and operation of the SMS	NA
7.5.4	Processes of the organization's SMS	8 Process Template
7.5.4	Records required to demonstrate evidence of conformity to the requirements of the standard and the organization's SMS	NA

The communication plan is an overview of what type of communication takes places, what the reason is, who is responsible for the communication, who the audience is and when or how frequently communication takes place. The template contains a long list of examples that may be included in this communication plan. It makes sense to review this plan regularly in order to verify if communication at the various levels has taken place.

Other types of documented information that it may be necessary to create, which are relevant to the particular SMS that your organization needs, are not mentioned in the standard. These documents may be internal or external in origin. It is up to your organization itself to determine what documentation is to be maintained in this area.

All processes used in the SMS need to be documented – this will be discussed in far more detail in the next section where most of the processes are mentioned. A generic Process Template has been provided in the toolkit.

Section 7.5.4 requires you to provide any records that illustrate conformity to the requirements of the standard. This is a very broad category, most of which is already covered by the mandatory documented information in the standard. It can, however, be extended with records such as meeting minutes, presentations from top management spreading awareness, risk acceptances, action lists and any other records generated during the course of developing, implementing, operating and improving the SMS.

5.5 CLAUSE 8

Clause 8 of ISO/IEC 20000-1 contains all the areas usually known as service management processes or practices. It is, therefore, obligatory that we start this section with a description of process design in general.

This section is based on the principles of Lean, which go far beyond the strict requirements of the standard but are generally useful as a framework for good process design. Keep in mind that any documentation of processes that suit your organization is sufficient to conform to the requirements of the standard. Processes that are documented only as drawings (for use by illiterate employees) have been used in some organization's SMS, for instance.

5.5.1 Process design

The definition of a process in ISO/IEC 20000-1 is as follows (see Clause 3.1.18):

"Process
set of interrelated or interacting activities that use inputs to deliver an intended result".

When you design a process according to Lean practices, you should start by considering what the inputs to the process are and what the outputs of the process are. More specifically, consider the SIPOC model: inputs are provided by a supplier (this is not the same as what is meant in the context of supplier management, but refers to anyone who provides inputs to a process), outputs are consumed by a customer (not necessarily the same as the customer using the services). This results in the following model:

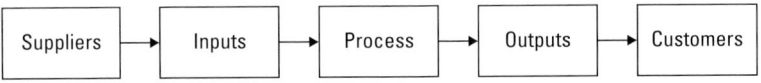

Figure 2. SIPOC Model

For each of your processes, you should start by creating a SIPOC and detailing the process that effectively transform the inputs into outputs. For instance, for a continual improvement process, the SIPOC as presented in Figure 3 was created.

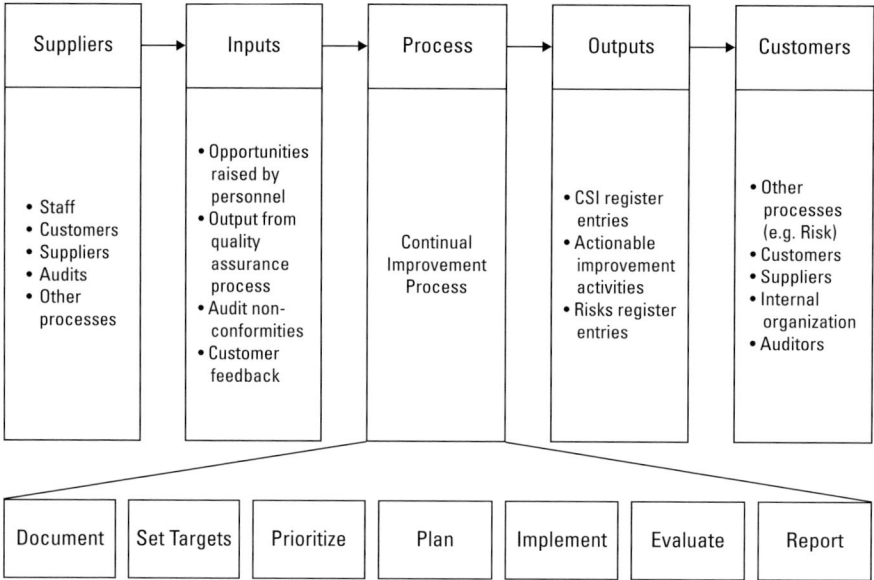

Figure 3. SIPOC for a continual improvement process

The output of one process can become the input of another: for instance, in *Figure 3*, the continual service improvement process uses the output from a quality assurance process as one of its inputs. In turn, one of the outputs of the continual service improvement process serves as an input to the risk management process. In this way, a complete system of interdependent processes can be mapped that show how each process relates to the other. An example of a system flow chart is illustrated in Figure 4.

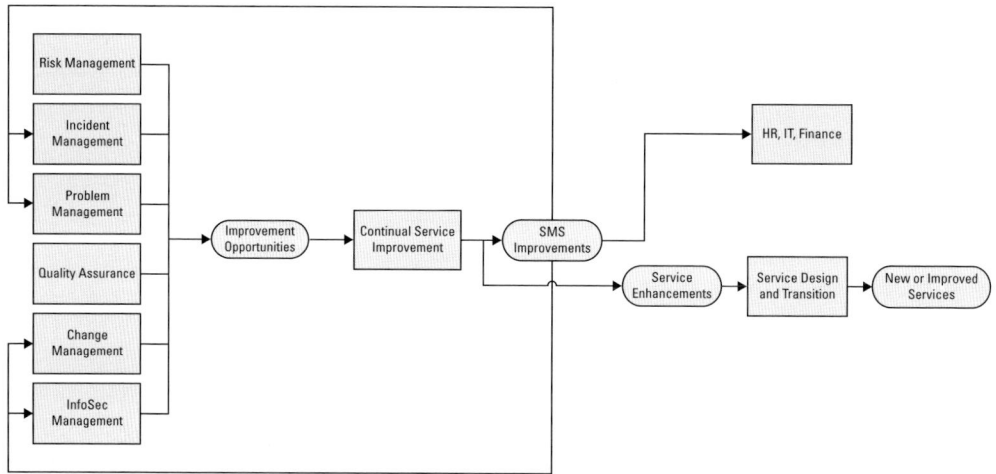

Figure 4. System flow chart based on a CSI process

The next level of detail for a process design is a detailed flow chart: the SIPOC show a handful of steps (seven, in case of the CSI process in *Figure 3*), but the detailed flow chart is able to show more details regarding the workings of the process, owners of steps and decisions made during the process. This may result in something similar to Figure 5.

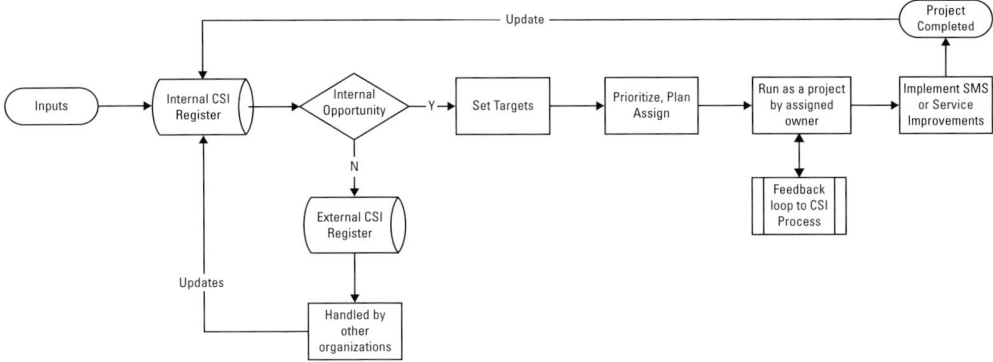

Figure 5. Detailed process flow for a CSI process

To complete the process design, a RACI Matrix should be created that shows the roles that are **A**ccountable for, **R**esponsible for, **C**onsulted on, and **I**nformed about the process. A RACI for the abovementioned CSI process is shown in Table 2.

Table 2. RACI Matrix for a ticket review process

Activity	Process Owner	Specialists	Service Manager	Managing Director	External Requestors
Process Management	R	R	A	C	C
CSI handling – overall	AR				
CSI handling – specific teams	A	R			
Monthly Report Generation	R		AR	I	
Recommendations and Feedback	AR	R	I	I	I
Tool Selection	R	R	AR	R	

All the above-mentioned elements come back in the *Process template* in the Documentation Toolkit, which can be used for the documentation of all processes in the SMS, including the following from Clause 8 of the standard.

5.5.2 Operational planning and control
Mandatory documented information

Clause	Document	Template
8.1	Documented information to the extent necessary to have confidence that processes have been carried out as planned	NA

This requirement means that you should be able to measure the processes to see if they have been performed well. You can think of setting process performance indicators that are measurable and producing monthly reports on these. This also serves as input to top management, giving them an indication that the SMS is running well.

5.5.3 Plan the services
Mandatory documented information

Clause	Document	Template
8.2.2	Service requirements	8.2.2 Service Requirements

Service requirements are usually documented at the beginning of developing a service. These requirements can be in any form – a simple document is sufficient, as long as it is available to the staff needing to refer to these requirements. This also needs to be done for existing services and any changes to services.

5.5.4 Control of parties involved in the service lifecycle
Mandatory documented information

Clause	Document	Template
8.2.3	Services and service components that are provided or operated by other parties	8.2.3 Other Parties
8.2.3	Processes, or parts of processes, in the organization's SMS that are operated by other parties	8.2.3 Other Parties
8.2.3	Definition of relevant controls for other parties involved in the service lifecycle	8.2.3 Other Parties

Where other parties, such as internal or external suppliers or customers acting as suppliers, are used in order to provide services, service components or (parts of) processes, this should be registered in the Other Parties spreadsheet. This is a simple list containing the name of the service/process, identifying what component is provided by a third party, the name of the third party and an identification of a control (e.g. contract, internal agreement, performance indicator) for the performance of the third party.

5.5.5 Service catalogue management
Mandatory documented information

Clause	Document	Template
8.2.4	Service Catalogue	8.2.4 Service Catalogue.xlsx

A service catalogue can provide a fairly simple list of the services, including their outcomes and possible dependencies on others. The template also contains fields for a unique identifier, a Service Owner and the status of the service (namely Active, Planned or Decommissioned). Note that the status may not always be relevant for customers, so you can omit this if you would like to keep the information internal.

5.5.6 Configuration management
Mandatory documented information

Clause	Document	Template
8.2.6	Definition of types of CIs	8.2.6 Configuration Items.xlsx
8.2.6	Configuration Information	8.2.6 Configuration Items.xlsx

Configuration items (CIs) are to be listed including a unique identifier, the type (e.g. software, hardware, tool, etc.), a description, a possible relationship with other CIs (e.g. when a CI is part of a larger CI, for instance an IP address on a server) and the status (active, decommissioned, planned). The spreadsheet in the toolkit can be utilized, but often, a Configuration Management Database (CMDB) is used, which forms a central repository for CI and configuration information.

Other configuration information relating to all CIs needs to be made available to other processes, such as change management. The format of this information can vary greatly depending on the type of CI, so no further template can be provided for this.

5.5.7 Business relationship management
Mandatory documented information

Clause	Document	Template
8.3.2	Customers, users, interested parties	8.3.2 Customers, users and other interested parties.docx
8.3.2	Service and customer complaints	8.3.2 Service complaints.xlsx
8.3.2	Customer Satisfaction	8 Report Template.pptx

A list of customers, users and other interested parties in the services needs to be created and maintained. This is a simple list, on which business relationship management activities can be recorded.

Complaints received about the services from customers or other stakeholders should be listed and acted on. The template provided has the following fields:
1. Reference number.
2. Name of the service involved.
3. Description of the service complaint.
4. Source of the complaint – e.g. the name of the user or customer.
5. Name of the service owner.
6. Follow-up actions to handle the complaint.
7. Closure date.
8. Status (open/closed).

5.5.8 Service level management
Mandatory documented information

Clause	Document	Template
8.3.3	Service Level Agreement	8.3.3 Service Level Agreement.docx
8.3.3	Performance against service level targets	8 Report Template.pptx
8.3.3	Workload changes	8 Report Template.pptx

For each service, a set of service level agreements (SLAs) should be developed. These should contain aspects such as service level targets, provider workload limits and any other exceptions. The template adds other possible information, such as penalties in cases where service levels are not met.

Performance against the service level targets and workload changes should be reported on, which can be completed with the default reporting template.

5.5.9 Supplier management
Mandatory documented information

Clause	Document	Template
8.3.4.1	Disputes with external suppliers	8.3.4 Disputes.xlsx
8.3.4.1	Contracts with external suppliers	8.3.4.1 Contract with External Suppliers
8.3.4.2	Agreements with internal suppliers or customers acting as suppliers	8.3.4.2 Agreement with Internal Suppliers or Customer acting as a Supplier

Supplier management information consists of legal documents, which may have a very specific form in your organization. The document templates provided for contracts and agreements with suppliers are based on the minimum requirements in ISO/IEC 20000-1, but may be superseded by what is already being used in your organization. Note that the contract with external suppliers requires more formal clauses than the agreement with internal suppliers or customers acting as suppliers.

Apart from these contracts and agreements, a list of possible disputes with suppliers needs to be maintained and acted on. The template contains the following fields:
1. Reference number.
2. Name of the service involved.
3. Supplier name.
4. Description of the dispute between the organization and the supplier.
5. Name of the service owner.
6. Any actions taken to resolve the dispute.
7. Closure date.
8. Status (open/closed).

5.5.10 Budgeting and accounting for services
Mandatory documented information

Clause	Document	Template
8.4.1	Costs against budget	8 Report Template.pptx

The only mandatory documented information in this section is a report on the costs incurred to provide the service and run the SMS versus the budget allocated. This report can come from your organization's default financial management system, outlining the financial forecasts that can be reviewed as well as any costs that can be managed, such as when the budget is at risk of being exceeded before the end of the budgeting period.

5.5.11 Demand management
Mandatory documented information

Clause	Document	Template
8.4.2	Demand and consumption of services	8 Report Template.pptx

The demand for services and their usage should be determined and forecasted. This can be done depending on your services, and is based on actual monitoring of the services and the customer requests for them.

5.5.12 Capacity management
Mandatory documented information

Clause	Document	Template
8.4.3	Capacity requirements	8.4.3 Capacity Requirements.docx

The requirements for service capacity can be documented in a table, which includes the following fields:
1. Service name.
2. Capacity type – human, technical, information or financial.
3. Current capacity.
4. Required capacity.
5. Date on which required capacity is to be implemented.
6. Possible impact of the capacity change on service level targets.

Capacity in ISO/IEC 20000-1 includes human, technical, information and financial resources. These are very different from each other and therefore each needs to be handled in its own way.

5.5.13 Change management
Mandatory documented information

Clause	Document	Template
8.5.1.1	Change Management Policy	8.5.1 Change Management Policy.docx
8.5.1.2	Requests for Change	8.5.1 Change Requests.xlsx
8.5.1.3	Analysis of RFCs	8 Report Template.pptx

Change management is an important area in service management, however the amount of information required to be documented is quite limited.

The Change Management Policy documents all services, components and other items that are governed by change management. It also defines the different types of change (e.g. Normal, Standard and Emergency) and how these should be managed in the organization. Finally, the policy highlights the criteria that determine what types of change may have a major impact on customers or the services. It is these major changes that will have to be run via the service design and transition process, which uses a more project-oriented approach than that needed for regular changes.

All change requests need to be documented. The template provided has the following fields:
1. Date on which request has been received.
2. Reference number.
3. Type of request – e.g. minor, major, removal, new service, etc.
4. Description of the change.
5. Date of last update.
6. Priority of the request.
7. Owner of the request, e.g. a change administrator.
8. An impact assessment of the change – this is to list the possible impact the change may have on services, customers, the business and finances.
9. Marker if this change needs to use the service design and transition process.
10. Due date for implementation.
11. Completion date.
12. Status (open/closed).

Based on the list of change requests that are compiled, reports can be put together that analyze trends in changes, e.g. increases in specific change types. If required, any opportunities for improvement may be derived from such a report.

5.5.14 Service design and transition
Mandatory documented information

Clause	Document	Template
8.5.2.2	Service Design	8.5.2 Service Design
8.5.2.3	Achievements against intended outcomes	8 Report Template.pptx

The service design and transition process is used as a project approach to manage changes that may have a major impact on the services or customers, as determined by the criteria set out in the Change Management Policy. Various other types of change however, also need to be run via this process, including new services, removal of services and transfers of services to a third party.

This process requires the production of a service design, which documents the service requirements, the approach to implementing it and any potential impacts on SLAs, contracts and the service catalogue.

5.5.15 Release and deployment management
Mandatory documented information

Clause	Document	Template
8.5.3	Results and conclusions drawn from the analysis of the success or failure of releases	8 Report Template.pptx
8.5.3	Acceptance criteria	8.5.3 Acceptance Criteria
8.5.3	Types of release	8.5.3 Types of Release

Reporting on the success or failure of releases should be regularly carried, for instance, every month. Any relevant statistics and root cause analysis can be documented in the default Report Template.

Acceptance criteria for releases are to be documented before the release is deployed into the live environment. It should then be verified against these acceptance criteria to see if they will be met so that the release can be approved and scheduled for deployment. If the acceptance criteria are not met, action needs to be taken to modify the release so that it can be approved, or the acceptance criteria may be modified if the customer or users agree with it. After deployment, tests should be performed to verify that the release does indeed meet the acceptance criteria when present in the live environment.

The types of release are defined in a simple list, where for each service the type of release is identified, e.g. normal, emergency, and others. Coupled with this, the way of managing the release types is determined, be it along the lines of standard change management and release or deployment processes for normal releases.

5.5.16 Incident management
Mandatory documented information

Clause	Document	Template
8.6.1	Incident records	8.6.1 Incidents.xlsx
8.6.1	Major incident procedure	8.6.1 Major Incident Procedure
8.6.1	Report on major incidents	8 Report Template.pptx

Incidents are likely to be managed using some form of (cloud-based) platform. For small organizations, however, a template has been provided with the minimum information needed to manage an incident. The fields are straightforward, as follows:
1. Date on which the incident was opened.
2. Type of incident – this can be by environment, by service, by CI type or other categories. Make sure information security incidents are indicated as such.
3. Incident description.
4. Reference number.
5. Date of last update.
6. Owner of the incident.
7. Impact of the incident on the services and/or the business on a scale of 1-5.
8. Urgency to resolve the incident on a scale of 1-5.
9. Priority of the incident – the multiplication of Impact and Urgency, so on a scale of 1-25.
10. Actions taken to deal with the incident.
11. Major incident indicator.
12. Due date for resolution of the incident.
13. Actual completion date.
14. Possible problem record opened in relation to this incident.
15. Status.

If a major incident occurs, a *Major Incident Procedure* should be in place that states how it should be handled. This procedure can indicate who needs to be involved, who takes the lead in managing the incident, how frequently certain levels of management need to be informed about progress, etc.

5.5.17 Service request management
Mandatory documented information

Clause	Document	Template
8.6.2	Service request records	8.6.2 Service Requests.xlsx
8.6.2	Instructions for the fulfilment of service requests	8.6.2 Service Request Work Instructions

Service requests are to be recorded, prioritized, fulfilled and closed. The spreadsheet provided has a number of fields that can be used to record service requests and track their progress, as follows:
1. Date on which the request was opened.
2. Request description.
3. Reference number.
4. Date of last update.
5. Priority of the request – this can be a High-Medium-Low scale or a numeric scale.
6. Owner of the request.
7. Actions taken to deal with the incident.
8. Due date for resolution of the incident.
9. Actual completion date.
10. Status (open/closed).

Each service request should have a documented procedure describing how to fulfil this. A framework for these procedures can be found in the Service Request Fulfilment Procedure Template. The exact procedure is dependent on the type of each request.

5.5.18 Problem management
Mandatory documented information

Clause	Document	Template
8.6.3	Problem records	8.6.3 Problems.xlsx
8.6.3	Known errors	8.6.3 Known Errors.xlsx
8.6.3	Report on effectiveness of problem resolution	8 Report Template.pptx

As with incidents, problems are likely to be managed using some form of (cloud-based) platform. For small organizations, a template has been provided with the minimum information needed to manage an incident, as follows:
1. Date on which the problem was opened.
2. Type of problem – this can be by environment, by service, by CI type or other categories.
3. Problem description.
4. Reference number.
5. Date of last update.
6. Priority of the problem – this can be a High-Medium-Low scale or a numeric scale.
7. Owner of the problem.
8. Impact of the problem on the services and/or the business.
9. Actions taken to deal with the problem.
10. Possible related incident records.
11. Possible related known errors.
12. Due date for resolution of the problem.
13. Actual completion date.
14. Status.

Known errors are issues with the services that have been raised, but for which no root cause has been determined. A workaround should have been established as part of the incident management process. Known errors can be documented in a spreadsheet, the template provided has the following fields:
1. Date on which the known error has been identified.
2. Reference number.
3. Description of the known error.
4. Date of last update.
5. Owner of the known error.
6. Impact of the error on the services.
7. Actions take to resolve the error, such as providing a workaround, or progress made in determining the root cause.
8. Related incident records.
9. Completion date – this is when the root cause has been determined and fixed.
10. Status (open/closed).

5.5.19 Service availability management
Mandatory documented information

Clause	Document	Template
8.7.1	Risks to service availability	6.1 Risk Register
8.7.1	Service availability requirements and targets	8.2.2 Service Requirements.docx
8.7.1	Service availability measurements report	8 Report Template.pptx

Use the general template for Service Requirements in Clause 8.2.2 to document service availability requirements as well, where requirements typically consist of a percentage availability of the service per month, such as 99.5%. This figure may exclude scheduled maintenance. Additional criteria can be set, such as no interruption in critical periods, be it month-end of year-end.

Based on service availability measurements, you can report historical availability using the generic Report Template.

5.5.20 Service continuity management
Mandatory documented information

Clause	Document	Template
8.7.2	Service continuity plan	8.7.2 Service Continuity Plan.docx
8.7.2	Service continuity procedure	8.7.2 Service Continuity Plan.docx
8.7.2	Risks to service continuity	6.1 Risk Register.xlsx
8.7.2	Results of service continuity tests	8.7.2 Service Continuity Plan.docx
8.7.2	Report on the cause, impact, and recovery when the service continuity plan(s) has been invoked	8 Report Template.pptx

The *Service Continuity Plan* needs to contain the following information:
- Criteria and responsibilities for invoking service continuity
- Procedures in the event of a major loss of service
- Targets for service availability when the service continuity plan is invoked
- Service recovery requirements
- Procedures for returning to normal working conditions
- Any results of service continuity tests can be documented in the plan as well.

In addition, risks to service continuity can be documented in the *Risk Register*.

Reporting on what caused a service continuity event, what the impact was and when the service continuity plan was invoked can be done using the generic *Report Template*.

5.5.21 Information security management
Mandatory documented information

Clause	Document	Template
8.7.3	Information security risks	6.1 Risk Register.xlsx
8.7.3	Decisions on information security controls	6.1 Risk Register.xlsx
8.7.3	Information security incidents	8.6.1 Incidents.xlsx
8.7.3	Report on information security incidents	8 Report Template.pptx
8.7.3	Information security policy	8.7.3 Information Security Policy.docx

Information security risks should be documented in the risk register and treated accordingly.

Controls implemented to mitigate information security risks should be decided on and noted in the risk register.

Information security incidents can be documented in the same register and treated according to the incident management process. This register can be used to report on information security controls as required.

The information security policy is a generic document, with the template provided using generic wording, which can be adapted as needed depending on what your organization needs.

■ 5.6 CLAUSE 9

Mandatory documented information

Clause	Document	Template
9.1	Results of monitoring, measurement, analysis and evaluation	See results required in other clauses
9.2	Audit program and results	9.2 Internal Audit Program.docx 9.2 Audit Report.docx
9.3	Management reviews	9.3 Management Reviews.docx
9.4	Report on effectiveness of the SMS and the services	See individual reports required in other clauses

5.6.1 Internal audit

An *internal audit program* should be created, which can typically take place once a year, or alternatively be broken into multiple sessions throughout the year. Qualified personnel should be responsible for these and have knowledge of the applicable standard for internal audits of management systems, ISO 19011. Note that this needs to be done irrespective of whether you want to have an external (certification) audit as well. The setup for this internal audit is described in the *Internal audit program* template. The deliverable of an internal audit is the *Audit Report*.

5.6.2 Management reviews

Management reviews should be held at least once a year, though twice is preferable. The aim of these reviews is to keep top management informed about the state of the SMS and the services. The input to the management review comes primarily from other documented information that you should already be maintaining, such as the risk register and measurements of processes and services. The management review is an executive summary of these operational documents, so should not go into full detail but rather cover the main points and overall trends. The template provided is an outline with guidance of the required sections of the management review.

5.7 CLAUSE 10

Mandatory documented information

Clause	Document	Template
10.1	Nonconformities and actions taken	10.1 Nonconformities.xlsx
10.2	Opportunities for improvement and implemented improvements	10.2 CSI Register.xlsx

The list of nonconformities is based on (internal) audit findings. The template is a simple spreadsheet with a reference number, description of the nonconformity, owner, due date, action log, completion date and status.

The CSI Register is based on any opportunities for improvement that have been raised as outputs from processes, a formalized continual service improvement plan, risks, and other sources of improvements. The template is a simple spreadsheet with a reference number, description of the CSI opportunity, owner, due date, action log, completion date and status.

6
Implementing the requirements of ISO/IEC 20000-1:2018 Running the SMS and the services

The success of running an SMS and providing services is not guaranteed by simply being able to produce documented information such as that described in the previous chapter. The reality is that a successful SMS is consistently integrated into the daily operation of a service provider, with documented information only being a product of the daily operation. This chapter addresses the practical aspects of running an SMS and it associated services, from planning through implementation and operation, to evaluation and continual improvement. It is not completely coincidental that these phases reflect the Deming Cycle (Plan-Do-Check-Act, PDCA), because, even though the explicit use of PDCA is no longer in the standard, the methodology still works as a simple framework that can be applied to the SMS and the services.

■ 6.1 PLANNING

6.1.1 Planning the SMS
Any initiative to start developing an SMS is almost always triggered by the need for a change in the way a service provider handles its services. This trigger can come from various sources:
- Internal needs to reorganize, reduce costs, or increase revenue;
- Customers may indicate that they want other features in their existing services, indicating dissatisfaction with their current service performance;
- Competitors may provide new services that eat away market share;
- Innovation, possibly triggered by the increased focus on digital transformation, may be initiated by the service provider itself.

Various improvement methodologies other than the Deming Cycle, such as Lean, Six Sigma, ITIL's seven step continual improvement process, or others, can trigger both the large- and small-scale improvements necessary in the services and existing service management practices. In any case, an SMS based on ISO/IEC 20000 will rarely be developed when no service management practices already exist. It will usually build on existing practices, however rudimentary, and improve these to meet service requirements.

Planning activities are responsible for most of the work involved in the implementation of an SMS. If planning is done well, operating, evaluating and improving the SMS become much easier. You should therefore spend a considerable amount of time in this planning phase, starting by creating a very high-level picture of what the SMS should look like. Take inspiration from Figure 1 in ISO/IEC 20000-1:2018, which shows the general outline of the requirements in the standard. Determine what this structure means for your organization and what the immediate activities are that you should initiate in order to plan the development.

The high-level activities outlined in Chapter 4 of this book indicate the planning activities needed. Creation of initial documentation, as discussed in Chapter 5 of this book, is another set of activities that will aid the planning process. However, it should be the actual service requirements where it all starts. As Clause 1.1 of ISO/IEC 20000-1 states, the aim of an SMS is to meet the service requirements and create value. You can only determine what these service requirements are and how the services can create value by asking the stakeholders of the SMS and the services: customers, suppliers, employees, management, supporting departments, etc. All should be listed as interested parties, and will have requirements for the SMS and the services that you need to consider in this planning phase. In particular:
- Customers will have requirements specific to the performance and availability of the services and effective support from the service provider.
- Suppliers will have requirements in terms of a smooth interaction between themselves and the service provider.
- Employees will have requirements for a set of effective processes that support them in their daily activities.

All interested parties have different ways of determining what value the SMS and the services create for them. Value can exist in terms of:
- Return on investment (the organization's top management);
- Effective support of the business outcomes (customers);
- Job satisfaction (employees);
- Fulfilment of commercial goals (suppliers).

Note that these examples of value are different for each stakeholder. Value co-creation (as used in some service management frameworks) is therefore never the creation of the same value by multiple stakeholders; instead, it is the simultaneous creation of different types of value for different stakeholders through the provision of the services. The practical activity required to identify service requirements and value creation consists of simply talking to these stakeholders and creating a list. The list of service requirements can then be prioritized and used for the planning of the SMS. This is not a one-time activity: PDCA is a cycle, meaning that you will continually move back to this planning phase and conduct this exercise over and again.

The prioritization of the service requirements and understanding value are activities that require the involvement of top management. It is clear from Clause 5 of the standard that top management needs to be involved in many steps during the complete lifecycle of the SMS and the services: after all, they are accountable for the success. In practice, this means that top management has an active role in the planning phase as well, by ensuring that all activities that are needed to establish the SMS are actually performed. This goes far beyond receiving a report regarding the progress of a project team that is establishing the SMS. It means getting actively involved where needed, for example by taking part in some sessions to prioritize service requirements, developing the service management policy and objectives, or actively contacting employees, customers and suppliers to listen to their opinions about the SMS and the services. Sometimes it makes sense for the team that is involved in the planning of the SMS to provide some explicit input to top management for them to communicate to the organization or other stakeholders. This can, for example, be in the form of talking points for town hall meetings or text used for internal or external communications to emphasize aspects such as policies, compliance, or the need for change. A good relationship with top management is indispensable in getting them involved with the SMS and the services at all stages. Active participation by top management is very important to emphasise the credibility of the efforts to plan and implement the SMS.

Three important parts of the SMS that top management should ensure are created are the service management policy, service management objectives and service management plan. The policy provides high-level guidance on the aims of the SMS, what top management wants to achieve with it, and their commitment to conform with the requirements that apply and improve when needed. The policy sets a framework for service management objectives, which can be part of an annual performance management cycle. These objectives are set in collaboration with all relevant stakeholders and are measurable performance targets for the SMS and the services. A plan should be created that outlines how these objectives are going to be met. The policy and objectives are inputs for the service management plan, together with the service requirements and other information. The plan unites all aspects of this planning phase and provides an overview of how the SMS and services will be operated, measured and improved, as well as what resources are going to be used to carry this out. In short, the service management policy describes *why* we need an SMS, the service management objectives describe *what* we are trying to achieve and the service management plan described *how* it is to be achieved.

Top management also has a responsibility to make resources available to run the SMS and the services. These resources consist of people, information, finances and technology.

People involved in the SMS should have the appropriate skills and experience for their jobs. It is important to do an initial assessment of the competences needed for different job roles that support the SMS and the services, so that people working in these roles can be appropriately trained. This assessment should be repeated regularly to ensure that possible changes in the SMS and the services are reflected in the competences of the people supporting them. This applies to all roles, including service desk agents, team leaders, managers, process owners, analysts, etc.

One of the most important information resources is knowledge, consisting of both documented information, such as the documentation discussed in Chapter 5 of this book or other documents not required by the standard that are still needed to run the SMS and the services, and institutional knowledge, which mostly exists in people's heads. ISO/IEC 20000 requires documented information to be managed and knowledge to be made available to all interested parties that need it. It therefore makes sense to set up a knowledge management system (which is a technological resource), that can range from a simple shared drive or cloud-based file sharing platform to extensive commercial knowledge management platforms. What is important is that the knowledge management system is appropriate for the organization and can be accessed by all stakeholders who need it – employees, suppliers, and in some cases customers.

What should not be forgotten is that the SMS does not exist in isolation from the rest of the company. In many cases, the scope of the SMS is limited to the part of a company that actually provides the services. There are, however, many other parts of the company that contribute to the service provider: for example, human resources, finance, sales, facilities and other teams will all contribute directly or indirectly to the SMS and are as such considered stakeholders. All these teams have their own business processes that influence what the SMS can or should look like. Part of the planning is therefore assessing what business processes have already been established that the SMS should align with and support. Sales will have specific targets for selling the services; therefore, the SMS and its processes should support them in doing so. Finance have their budgeting and accounting methodologies that will influence the way in which the SMS and the services are financially supported. Facilities provide a work environment that determines the way in which staff can operate to support the SMS and the services, while HR obviously has an influence on the human resources who are working to provide this support. These departments form bi-directional relationships, where the SMS is influenced by the business processes and vice versa. They need alignment to be able to support each other.

6.1.2 Planning processes

The process-side of planning the SMS consists of a number of different aspects. To start, governance is required to run the processes in an integrated manner. Governance here means that responsibilities are established and the processes themselves interact in an effective way. This can be ensured by the process owners using the three activities of Governance of IT from ISO/IEC 38500: Evaluate, Direct and Monitor. Through monitoring of the process outputs, these results can be evaluated, and management can direct the organization to improve the processes where required.

Responsibilities for processes are often allocated to a role called process owner or process manager. This role is responsible and/or accountable for the proper running of the process. It is all about leading the planning and documentation, making sure the process operates properly, and that the process is improved when required. Depending on the scope, a process owner can own multiple related processes. They regularly report on the performance of their process(-es) to top management.

Processes in the SMS need to interact so that they support the services: incident management and problem management are closely related and need to exchange information. Change management interacts with a range of other processes, such as configuration management, business relationship management and service level management. As indicated in Chapter 5 of this book, a system diagram can visualize the interaction of all these processes. More importantly, when processes are properly documented, the interaction with other processes should be made clear, for example, what outputs of this process serve as inputs to others? What inputs does this process require from other processes? These interactions should also be made clear to the staff working with these processes: the quality of their work not only determines the success of their own area, but also has an influence on other processes and eventually on the SMS, the services and the business outcomes.

This is part of the communication that needs to take place and the awareness that needs to be created among the staff. A service desk agent needs to identify how the information they receive from the customer about, for example, a service request should be registered in order for the request to be implemented. The possible information security impact of the request should be understood before it is fulfilled. Agreed service levels for the request need to be verified in order to set the right expectations with the customer.

Planning and designing the actual processes can start from using existing ones, even if nothing is documented as yet. Take these and determine, based on the service requirements and other inputs, what would need to be changed in order for these processes to be optimized. Consult various stakeholders who operate the process, or are otherwise involved, to gather their input and form agreements with them. If possible, try out the new processes in a small-scale pilot environment to see if they perform as expected. If so, use the guidance in Chapter 5 of this book to document them and roll them out in the rest of the organization. Make sure that the processes can be measured: the standard requires you to establish performance criteria for the processes and control them, meaning that you should be able to measure the performance of your processes and determine their effectiveness. These performance criteria can be determined based on the service requirements, the service management policy and the service management plan.

6.1.3 Planning working with other parties

Many services nowadays are based on components or processes provided by other suppliers. Think of an application service hosted on a third-party cloud platform; a transport service using planning software supplied by another software company; or simply the electronic payments done in any retail service, supplied by financial service providers. ISO/IEC 20000-1 has a significant focus on the use of suppliers in the SMS. A distinction is made between internal suppliers, customers acting as suppliers and external suppliers, with each having an impact on the level of control you need to exert on them. In all cases, it is you as the main service provider who remains accountable for the quality of the services, the value generated by them and the effectiveness of the SMS as a whole, even if all of these are areas where both suppliers and customers have specific responsibilities as well.

Planning to work with suppliers involves clarifying who provides what service component or runs what process; how these components or processes interact with the rest of the SMS and the services; and what service targets apply to service components or processes provided by other parties. This should all be contractually agreed in the case of external providers, because these are usually commercial agreements. In the case of internal suppliers, who are part of the same company that provides the services, or in the case of customers also acting as suppliers, with whom there is already a contract, using any agreement is sufficient.

The agreed service targets with customers are inputs for determining the service targets with suppliers. Say you provide an internet access service for which you agree that incidents will be resolved within four hours. If you have outsourced your technical field service to an external provider, you need to agree targets for fixing the parts under their responsibility that are clearly under four hours, otherwise you run the risk of exceeding the customer's SLA. Suppliers should be held accountable for meeting their part of the service targets.

ISO/IEC 20000-1 explicitly states that the service provider may not use suppliers to provide *all* services: you need to do something yourself, otherwise it is hard to show that you actually control any part of the service you provide to your customers.

ISO/IEC 20000-3 discusses the use of suppliers in greater detail, using various simple and complex examples.

■ 6.2 OPERATING

Once the planning phase has been completed, implementing and operating the SMS and the services should be relatively straightforward.

It should be noted that the implementation of a new or changed process can have a significant impact on the organization. This impact can range from updating documentation to making people aware of the new process; or updating systems or informing customers and other stakeholders about the impact of the change on their side. There are several Organizational Change Management methodologies (OCM, not to be confused with the operational change management process) that can be helpful here. For instance, John P. Kotter's enhanced eight-step change process is well-known. What is important for organizational change is to make sure that everyone involved understands the reasons behind it and the impact on their own role and activities. Top management should clearly support the change and communicate about it.

Communication is generally an important part of ISO/IEC 20000, encouraged to take place at all levels in the organization, starting with top management. It makes sense to create a communication plan listing all opportunities for communication about the SMS and the services. This plan can contain items such as team meetings, operational reviews, town hall meetings, formal presentations, email and face-to-face communication, etc. Make sure there is ample opportunity for interaction, since effective communication has to involve an exchange of perspectives, it is always a dialogue.

When operating the SMS and the services, there should be a continual focus on the effectiveness of the activities and the value generated by the services. At a process-level, this means that you should observe and measure the effectiveness of the processes and flag any issues that need to be improved. In almost every process area in Clause 8 of ISO/IEC 20000-1, there is a requirement regularly to verify if the objectives are still being met. This may involve verifying the accuracy of configuration information (configuration management), measuring satisfaction with the services (business relationship management), monitoring actual costs against the budget (budgeting and accounting for services), and monitoring capacity usage (capacity management), to name but a few. This not only needs to be carried out for individual processes, but also for the overall interaction and governance. The system map of the interaction of processes should be revisited regularly, particularly after changes have been made to individual processes, to ensure that the output of one process is still adequate to serve as the input for another. Roles and responsibilities may also have to change when the processes themselves change. For example, the automation of part of an incident management process may bring with it IT technical requirements for the process owner's role that go beyond the skills of the person currently appointed.

Apart from operating the processes, there is also the aspect of operating the rest of the SMS. This includes making sure that the necessary resources are still available to support the SMS: are there enough staff to support the SMS and the services? Are staff sufficiently competent? Sometimes new staff are hired to replace people leaving the company and these new appointees need to go through an extensive training program to be able to perform their tasks. This can leave a gap of sometimes several weeks during which human resources are at a low level, which may in turn impact the effectiveness of the SMS and the quality of the services. Similarly, changes to services may lead to changes in job descriptions and the required skills. These changes may trigger educational needs for existing staff or hiring needs to augment staff with skilled specialists. All these aspects need continuous monitoring and improvement as and when necessary.

Everything that was originally planned for the establishment of the SMS and the services will, at some point in time, no longer be adequate, given that service requirements, the marketplace and customer expectations change. The continuous cycle of monitoring this adequacy during the operation of the SMS and the services includes reviewing the service management policy, objectives and plan. These should, therefore, be reviewed with some regularity by top management, updated and communicated where necessary. Opportunities to do so exist at the beginning of the year, when organizational performance targets are usually set, but also during management reviews, after major incidents or after meeting important customers. This also applies to the alignment of the SMS with the business processes and outcomes as discussed under the planning section. This alignment has two perspectives: the business perspective and the SMS and service perspective. Changes on one side may require re-evaluation and re-alignment on the other. The business may want to change the nature of the services it provides to its customers, which has an obvious major impact on the SMS and the services. On the other hand, changes made in, for example, staffing levels or service levels for the SMS and the services may impact the business and re-alignment may be required there.

In the list of process areas in Clause 8 of the standard, there is a large area relating to major changes made to the services: Design and transition of new and changed services. This process area had a complete clause of its own in the 2011 edition of ISO/IEC 20000-1 but has now found a place among the other service management processes. However, this does not mean it is regarded as any less important. Changes that have a major impact on customers or other services, the introduction of new, or removal or, transfers of services, and any other major changes all have a specific set of requirements in the standard that indicate they require specific attention. A more project-based approach is required for these, which includes:
- gathering requirements from customers, suppliers and other stakeholders;
- coming up with a proper service design based on these requirements;
- undertaking a risk assessment on the impact of these major changes to other services;
- determining the resource requirements and other impact on all aspects of the SMS; and
- establishing the impact on customers and other interested parties.

These are in fact aspects of planning, design, transition, evaluation and improvement in this process area, so the complete Deming Cycle applies.

■ 6.3 EVALUATING

Evaluation of the SMS and the services is mostly addressed in Clause 9 of the standard and consists of three elements: reporting, management review and internal audit.

Reporting includes activities to monitor, analyze and evaluate the SMS and the services. Many clauses of ISO/IEC 20000-1 explicitly mention that reports should be created, performance analyzed, or effectiveness evaluated. Much of this can be done with the help of commercial service management platforms that gather the data on incidents, changes and service requests, and can create default graphs regarding volumes, timeliness, quality and other performance aspects. The output of such systems is necessarily limited though and may have to be augmented with data you gather elsewhere, or combined with data from other systems. For example, data from a capacity management system may have to be combined with data from a configuration management system to produce meaningful results of capacity usage for specific service components.

As mentioned before, process performance should be measured, analyzed and reported on, which may be challenging depending on the design of your processes. It is, therefore, important to consider measurement and reporting aspects in the planning phase of your processes and build the steps to measure process performance from the outset. Lean's value stream mapping is a powerful approach to do this, because it explicitly outlines what steps introduce delays or what are unnecessary steps in the process.

Reports are most powerful when presented in a graphical way, because this is usually much easier to understand than extensive tables or words. A graph or image, however, needs to be meaningful and appropriate to convey the message the report wishes to give. You also need to consider the audience for the report: a report about service performance aimed at top management needs to be much more generic than that aimed at staff running the processes. Similarly, a report for a customer or supplier may not contain information that is considered confidential by the service provider.

Risks should be reported on in various areas: these include risks to the SMS in general, to service availability and continuity, to information security, risks around service requirements, and risks regarding the use of suppliers, to name a few. These can be established in an integrated way if this is practical. Not all stakeholders need to be made aware of all of the risks. : operational risks may be treated by individual teams and may only need to be escalated to management or top management if their support or visibility of the risk is required. This layered approach to risk management and risk reporting makes sure that risks are dealt with at the appropriate level in the organization.

The management review (also called management system review, MSR) is an opportunity to have a discussion with top management about the state of the SMS and the services. There are a significant number of topics that the standard requires you to cover in this review: service performance, changes to the SMS, opportunities for improvement, resource needs, etc. It is very much dependent on the organization and how often such reviews are held. Sometimes this can be an annual review, whilst at other times it happens quarterly. There are also organizations that integrate these reviews into their operational meetings, so that topics of the management review simply refer to discussions that were held in previews meetings. The importance of the management review is that top management is continually kept informed about the SMS and the services and can make any necessary decisions based on that information. It is also an opportunity for them to express their opinion and provide direction to the organization.

Even if you don't use ISO/IEC 20000 to become certified through an external audit, you are still required to have an internal audit program. This program can be set up in various ways: it often takes just a sample of the SMS, simply because evaluating all aspects of it can be very time-consuming. Within a certain period, however, all aspects of the SMS should be audited, either through a single, large audit, or via a series of smaller ones. The internal auditor needs to be independent of the organization that is being audited, otherwise there may be conflicts of interest, since the auditor needs to be able to take a neutral position in order to evaluate the SMS. Results of the audits serve as input to the management review.

■ 6.4 IMPROVING

The final phase of the Deming Cycle, before you return to the beginning, is Act, which involves improving the SMS and the services based on various sources of input. You should already have your measurements relating to process performance and the effectiveness of the SMS and the services, as described in the previous section. Feedback from customer satisfaction surveys, employee satisfaction surveys and other stakeholder surveys will help determine more areas that may have to be improved.

A way to generate opportunities from the teams involved in supporting the SMS and the services is to regularly ask them what issues arise while doing their jobs. These discussions can often result in actionable improvement opportunities. Finally, the risk management process will certainly generate actions that need to be taken to address specific risks.

All this feedback should be fed into a continual improvement process that evaluates, prioritizes, and executes these improvement opportunities.

Continual improvement can be set up using a number of simple tools: for example, a Kanban-board listing opportunities in their various stages – To-do, In Progress, and Completed; or a simple spreadsheet with a list of improvement opportunities which you can prioritize and allocate to people to work on; or even a commercial platform that allows you to do the same things in an electronic or cloud-based way. The point is that improvement opportunities should be registered, prioritized, allocated to the right people to execute and then tracked to completion.

A separate category of improvements mentioned in the standard is nonconformities. These are aspects of the SMS that do not conform to the requirements in ISO/IEC 20000-1. These may come up during internal or external audits, or during the operation of the SMS. Nonconformities need to be corrected as soon as possible if you want to conform to the standard and this is achieved using the continual improvement process as described above. Nonconformities are items that need to be discussed in management reviews, as described in the previous section, and will therefore receive top management attention. To close off non-conformities, the effectiveness of measures taken to deal with them needs to be verified, so that you can be sure these non-conformities will not reoccur.

Even though this step of improving might seem to be the final one, it actually leads towards starting the Deming Cycle all over again: improvements that need to be made to the SMS and services will in many cases mean a return to the planning stage, which is needed to coordinate the implementation of the improvements in such a way that the SMS and the services are not negatively impacted. In this way, the circle is closed and the process of planning, implementing, operating, evaluating and improving the SMS and the services is itself a process of continual learning and development.

7 Certification

Most organizations will want to implement the requirements of ISO/IEC 20000-1 to primarily improve their existing service management practices, with the aim of:
- Creating greater efficiency internally;
- Reducing costs (and becoming more profitable, if your organization is a for-profit one);
- Improving service quality;
- Increasing customer satisfaction through enhancing the value they experience from your services.

If, however, you want to demonstrate externally that this is in fact the case and that you conform to all the requirements in ISO/IEC 20000-1, then you will need to go through a certification process with an external audit.

An audit is an assessment of conformance with the requirements of the standard or, as it states, for *"an organization to demonstrate its capability for the planning, design, transition, delivery and improvement of service"*. It is therefore an opportunity for you to show off how well you are running your SMS. This requires a certain amount of documented information, as required by the standard (see chapter 5 of this book), together with a level of confidence and knowledge inside the organization to be able to communicate this to the auditor.

The main points to keep in mind when opting for an external audit to gain certification are:
- Make sure you don't polish up your ways of working just for the audit — show the day-to-day way of working of your SMS instead;
- See an audit as a learning experience: it is not a sign of failure when you get feedback from the auditor that something does not meet the requirements; rather it is an opportunity for you to improve your SMS;
- Do make people aware that the audit is taking place and make sure they can talk with the auditor if required.

The basic requirements to get certified are as follows:
- Conformance with ISO/IEC 20000-1:2018;
- A successful audit performed by an auditor who works for an accredited certification body. Note that there are auditors who work for organizations that are not accredited, and while these audits may be good, without accreditation they cannot be verified to conform to the requirements for certification bodies.

The audit process itself runs in two phases: a Stage 1 (Intent) audit and a Stage 2 (Implementation) audit. Sometimes these are preceded by a Pre-audit, but it is not mandatory to perform this.

The Stage 1 audit is somewhat high-level and often conducted remotely, looking mostly at what is in place in relation to documentation, including policies, scope and processes. It will also ensure that there is top management commitment. From this audit, a number of potential nonconformities or opportunities for improvement may emerge that you will need to address before the Stage 2 audit commences.

The Stage 2 audit is a full on-site audit of the actual day-to-day functioning of the SMS. This is not necessarily a sample of the SMS as a whole but it will cover all clauses in ISO/IEC 20000-1. This audit can result in (major or minor) nonconformities and opportunities for improvement. Opportunities for improvement are not failures to conform to the requirements of the standard, but optional aspects that can be improved. Non-conformities, however, need to be addressed within a certain period of time following the Stage 2 audit. Once resolved, the auditor will present a recommendation to the certification body to provide your organization with the ISO/IEC 20000-1 certificate. Ultimately, it is the certification body that decides on this, not the auditor himself.

Your certificate will state the scope of your SMS and have the seals of both the certification body and the accreditation body (authorized by the International Accreditation Forum (IAF) or European Co-operation for Accreditation (EA).

To find out more about certification, speak to an accredited certification body.

8 Beyond ISO/IEC 20000

So, you are now certified — congratulations! Do you think you have achieved the final level of maturity for your service management practices? It's unlikely, since ISO/IEC 20000-1 only aims to provide the minimum requirements for an SMS, which demonstrates to your customers that your SMS is at an internationally agreed level, indicating that it is under good management.

But there is always room for improvement — not only in terms of continual improvement, but also in the way that service management is seen by service providers. Two recent publications seek to expand this perspective and adapt its practices to the needs of today's services, service providers and their customers.

■ 8.1 VERISM

VeriSM™ [15] extends service management beyond just IT, which traditional IT service management often still focuses on, to the organization as a whole. VeriSM states that all departments in the organization contribute to the success of services, including HR, Finance and other departments that are typically further away from the services themselves. Based on this assertion, VeriSM innovates service management by defining a model that includes a Management Mesh: this is a flexible structure based on the Resources, Environment, Management Practices and (Emerging) Technologies that a service provider can use. For a given service the organization might, for instance, choose to use DevOps as a Management Practice and virtualization as an Emerging Technology, but for other services it may opt to use a combination of Lean management and cloud-based technologies. The VeriSM model provides this flexibility, which can underpin your ISO/IEC 20000 (or other) service management system.

8.2 THE ISMF

The Integral Service Management Framework (ISMF) as described in the book *Service Management: It's all about the People* [16] provides a psychological perspective on service management. It provides a framework that looks at the organization and service management from four basic perspectives: People's Attitude, Knowledge and Emotions; People's Behaviour; the Organization's Culture; and the Organization's Structure. In all four areas, there is the possibility to grow or mature the organization and the SMS will mature along with it. Essentially, a mature organization can support a more mature SMS that can provide services at a more mature level, thus increasing customer satisfaction.

These are two important publications that suggest service management does not need to be a static body of knowledge, but can evolve dynamically with new insights, new technologies, new practices and new demands from customers.

Appendix A
ISO/IEC 20000 resources

Note: ISO standards listed below refer to the latest versions. Check on iso.org for the most current version of standards.

[1] ISO/IEC 20000-1, Information technology — Service management – Part 1: Service management system requirements

[2] ISO/IEC 20000-2, Information technology — Service management — Part 2: Guidance on the application of service management systems

[3] ISO/IEC 20000-3, Information technology — Service management — Part 3: Guidance on scope definition and applicability of ISO/IEC 20000-1

[4] ISO/IEC 20000-5, Information technology — Service management — Part 5: Exemplar implementation plan

[5] ISO/IEC 20000-6, Information technology — Service management — Part 6: Requirements for bodies providing audit and certification of service management systems

[6] ISO/IEC TR 20000-7, Information technology — Service management — Part 7: Guidance on the integration and correlation of ISO/IEC 20000-1:2018 to ISO 9001:2015 and ISO/IEC 27001:2013

[7] ISO/IEC 20000-10, Information technology — Service management — Part 10: Concepts and terminology

[8] ISO/IEC TR 20000-11, Information technology — Service management — Part 11: Guidance on the relationship between ISO/IEC 20000-1 and service management frameworks: ITIL®

[9] ISO/IEC TR 20000-12, Information technology — Service management — Part 12 Guidance on the relationship between ISO/IEC 20000-1 and service management frameworks: CMMI-SVC®

[10] ISO/IEC TR 20000-13, Information technology — Service management — Part 13 Guidance on the relationship between ISO/IEC 20000-1 and service management frameworks: COBIT

[11] A Practical Guide – ISO/IEC 20000-1 – IT Service Management, ISO, 2019

[12] ISO 9001, Quality management systems — Requirements

[13] ISO/IEC 27001, Information technology — Security techniques — Information security management systems — Requirements

[14] ISO 19011 — Guidelines for auditing management systems
[15] Agutter, Claire et al., *VeriSM™, a Service Management Approach for the Digital Age.* Van Haren Publishing, 2017
[16] Van der Haven, Dolf J.H., *Service Management: It's all about the People.* ITSM Press, 2018
[17] ISO/IEC 38500 – Information technology – Governance of IT for the organization

Appendix B
Differences between the 2011 and the 2018 editions of ISO/IEC 20000-1

■ INTRODUCTION

This section outlines the main differences between the previous version of ISO/IEC 20000-1, published in 2011, and the 2018 edition. For ease of reference, these will be referred to throughout as "the 2011 edition" and "the 2018 edition".

The 2018 edition has undergone significant structural changes as well as some content changes. The aim of the update was to reduce the amount of required documented information, provide more alignment with current developments in service management, such as DevOps, Agile and Service Integration and Management (SIAM), and facilitate integration with other management systems standards.

■ MANAGEMENT SYSTEMS STANDARDS STRUCTURE

The 2018 edition has adopted the high-level structure for management system standards, referred to as "Annex SL". Annex SL provides a common structure, some requirements, and common terms and definitions for management system standards. This makes it easier to integrate the implementation of ISO/IEC 20000-1 with other management system standards, such as ISO 9001, or ISO/IEC 27001.

As a result, the 2018 edition has the same ten-clause structure as many other management system standards:
Clause 1 - Scope
Clause 2 - Normative references
Clause 3 - Terms and definitions
Clause 4 - Context of the organization
Clause 5 - Leadership
Clause 6 - Planning
Clause 7 - Support of the SMS

Clause 8 - Operation of the SMS
Clause 9 - Performance evaluation
Clause 10 - Improvement

Terms and definitions are in Part 1 as well as Part 10. Part 10 contains additional terms and definitions for terms not used in part 1, such as governing body, which are used in the guidance. Part 10 also includes an introduction to the ISO/IEC 20000 series, an explanation of all of the parts and of related standards.

Furthermore, ISO/IEC 20000-1 now shares common definitions and text with other management system standards, further facilitating integration between them. Many terms have had updated definitions, there are some new terms from Annex SL and some new terms specific to ISO/IEC 20000-1. Some terms from the 2011 edition have been deleted. The key terms that have been revised since the 2011 edition include:

- *Organization* is now used in places where the 2011 edition would have used *service provider*. This is in alignment with other management system standards;
- *Documented information* is now used instead of *documentation*;
- *External supplier* is used instead of *supplier*;
- *Internal supplier* is used instead of *internal group*;
- *Service availability* is used instead of *availability*;
- *Configuration information* is used instead of *Configuration management database* (CMDB).

■ EXPLANATION OF DIFFERENCES

General requirements

Clause 4 requires the organization to conduct the following (in addition to what was already in Clause 4 of the 2011 edition), *SMS General Requirements*:
1. Determine internal and external issues influencing its purpose and the intended outcomes of the SMS.
2. Identify any interested parties and their requirements that are relevant to the SMS and the services provided.

Clause 5 Leadership asks for similar provisions from top management as the 2011 edition, with an additional focus on determining what constitutes value for the organization and its customers, promoting continual improvement and the integration of the SMS and its associated policy and objectives with the business outcomes of the organization.

Instead of a management representative, the 2018 edition now requires general assignments of roles, responsibilities and authorities in order to make sure the SMS conforms to the standard's requirements and that top management is kept informed about the performance of the SMS and the services.

Clause 6 Planning covers risk management, defining service management objectives and planning of the SMS. Risk management was in the 2011 edition but is more extensive in 2018. The organization's internal and external issues as well as the requirements of interested parties need to be taken into account to determine and treat risks to the SMS while establishing continual improvement. The organization needs to assess its own risk appetite in these areas and define risk treatment actions in its planning of the SMS. Opportunities also need to be considered and addressed.

The service management objectives are more specific than the 2011 edition and require planning for how to achieve them.

Planning the SMS in the 2018 edition aligns to Clause 4.5.2 Plan the SMS in the 2011 edition. There are some minor changes here.

Clause 7 provides requirements for the support of the SMS, including resources, communication, competency, awareness, documentation and knowledge management. Communication requirements are largely new to the 2018 edition as this was limited in the 2011 edition. Clause 7.6 Knowledge is new and requires the organization to determine what is needed to support the SMS and the services, and how this knowledge is maintained and made available.

Clause 8 deals with the operation of the SMS and includes all the processes formerly covered in Sections 5 to 9 of the 2011 edition. These will be dealt with in more detail in the following section.

In Clause 9, all requirements related to performance evaluation have been combined, including monitoring, auditing, management reviews and service reporting. The requirements for monitoring, measuring, analyzing and evaluating are largely new to the 2018 edition. Service reporting, from Clause 6.2 of the 2011 edition, has been moved to Clause 9.4 of the 2018 edition covering the general requirements of reporting. But the actual production of reports has been moved into the relevant clauses of the standard. The requirements for nonconformity and corrective action in Clause 10.1 of the 2018 edition are largely new.

Service management processes

Clause 8 in the 2018 edition contains the activities that are commonly referred to as service management processes, although in practice organizations may split them, combine them or call them something else.

Changes in requirements of these sub-clauses are as follows.

Operational planning and control
This is largely an Annex SL clause regarding planning, operating and controlling the processes to meet the requirements and action plans made in Clause 6.

Service delivery
This is a small section requiring coordination and execution of the activities needed to deliver the services, which aligns to Clause 4.5.3 (Implement and operate the SMS [Do]) in the 2011 edition.

Plan the services
This new section requires appropriate planning for services and alignment of these with the service management policy and objectives, as well as the business needs. The needs of the organization and other interested parties need to be considered here as well, with the only requirement from the 2011 edition being the need to gather service requirements.

Service catalogue management
This is a new activity area, but some requirements were present in the 2011 edition in Clause 6.1 Service level management. This section is now more explicit about what should be described in the service catalogue, including who should be able to benefit from and access it.

Asset management
Asset management requires service assets to be managed in line with legal, regulatory and contractual requirements, largely taken from the requirements for the management representative in the 2011 edition.

Configuration management
Configuration management has been simplified, now focusing on the definition and management of CIs, but not requiring a CMDB or an explicit configuration management procedure.

Business relationship management
The 2018 edition's requirements for business relationship management are fairly similar to those published in 2011.
The review has been clarified as covering the performance trends and outcome of the services to clearly distinguish it from the more operational review in service level management. The complaints requirements have been simplified.

Service level management
SLM now excludes the service catalogue management elements, as these have been moved to Clause 8.2.2 Service catalogue management. Requirements for managing

internal groups (now called internal suppliers) and customers acting as suppliers have been moved to supplier management.

Supplier management
Supplier management now makes a distinction between management of internal suppliers and customers acting as suppliers, and external suppliers. The contractual requirements for external suppliers have been reduced.
When dealing with other parties, such as internal or external suppliers or customers acting as suppliers, the word governance has been dropped to avoid confusion with governance of organizations or governance of IT. Instead, Clause 8.2.3 refers to control of other parties involved in the service lifecycle. This clause has significant changes from the 2011 edition. Management of internal and external suppliers as well customers acting as suppliers is covered in 8.3.4 supplier management.

Budgeting and accounting for services
Budgeting and accounting have been simplified to encourage budgeting and accounting for services to follow the organization's overall financial management processes. This now allows for budgeting for a service or group of services.

Demand management
This new section introduces the requirement to determine current and forecast future demand for services as well as monitoring and reporting the consumption. It is partly taken from the 2011 edition of capacity management.

Capacity management
Capacity management focuses on the capacity of all types of resources, including human, financial, and technical information. It works closely with demand management to deliver the required capacity for services. The requirement for a capacity plan has been removed and replaced with the requirement to plan capacity with a reduced list of items.

Change management
The change management clause has been split into policy, initiation and activities. The change management policy has been clarified and added to, with categories of change being explicitly specified to run via service design and transition due to the impact on the service, customers or other factors.

Service design and transition
Service design and transition was called the design and transition of new and changed services process in the 2011 edition. This area has been significantly streamlined and made easier to understand. The current structure has three parts: plan, design, and build and transition.

Release and deployment management
The release and deployment policy has been replaced by the need to define the types of release, their frequency and how they are to be managed. The requirements have been reduced to avoid overlap with change management.

Incident management
This section has been split from the combined process with service request fulfilment in the 2011 edition. Requirements for incidents are similar as before.

Service request management
Service requests are handled similarly to incidents, but the requirements have been simplified from the 2011 edition.

Problem management
Requirements for problem management are similar to the 2011 edition.

Service availability management
Service availability management requirements have been simplified, now focusing on risk assessment, fulfilling requirements for availability, monitoring availability and dealing with availability incidents. The service availability plan is no longer needed.

Service continuity management
Service continuity management requirements are in line with the original 2011 edition.

Information security management
The information security requirements have been simplified from the 2011 edition to remove the need for information security objectives, information security risk approach and acceptance criteria, and an information security audit.

About the author

Dolf van der Haven was born in Muiderberg, the Netherlands, in 1971. Originally a Geophysicist, he has a broad background in IT, telecommunications, management, psychotherapy and service management. He currently works as a Service, Quality and Information Security Management Consultant at Verizon Enterprise Solutions and is Co-founder and Managing Director of Powerful Answers, a service management consultancy based in Bulgaria, the Netherlands and the Czech Republic. He is also a member of ISO/IEC Joint Technical Committee 1, Subcommittee 40, which develops the ISO/IEC standard series 20000 (Service Management) and 38500 (Governance of IT), among others.

Previous publications include *The Healing Elephant* (2008 in Dutch, 2009 in English), about psychotherapy; *The Human Face of Management* (2014) about people management; *Service Management – It's all about the People* (2018) about service management; *An Introduction to ISO/IEC 38500* (2018) about Governance of IT.

Dolf lives in Groenekan, the Netherlands, with his partner and their 150 chickens.